ENGLISH LITERATURE

CLEP* Test Study Guide

© 2021 Breely Crush Publishing, LLC

*CLEP is a registered trademark of the College Entrance Examination Board which does not endorse this book.

971010221143

Published by Breely Crush Publishing, LLC
10808 River Front Parkway
South Jordan, UT 84095
www.breelycrushpublishing.com

ISBN-10: 1-61433-785-3
ISBN-13: 978-1-61433-785-0

Printed and bound in the United States of America.

Table of Contents

 Introduction

The study of English Literature is not a narrow field. It covers an expansive time period beginning with the writing of Beowulf before the 10th century A.D. and continuing with modern poets and novelists. English Literature includes a wide assortment of authors, including William Shakespeare, Edgar Allan Poe, Sylvia Plath, and Toni Morrison. Plus, it covers an array of universal themes.

In order to discuss all of the different elements, one must first understand the terminology used to discuss literature.

Literature Terminology

Evaluating any piece of literature requires that you be able to talk about certain elements of the work. These elements allow people to talk about the story in terms that each of them can understand in the same way that medical terminology allows doctors to talk about their patients' conditions. The first set of terms that you should be familiar with are listed below:

 Plot

The term "plot" refers to the series of connected events within the piece of literature. While there are different ways to construct an effective plot, one of the most common consists of the following parts:

- Complication – Conflict between the main characters is building.

- Turning Point – At this point, the main character has reached his or her apex of good fortune in the story.

- Denouement – Things begin to go downhill for the main character. Painful or shocking discoveries are often part of the denouement.

- Resolution – By the work's end there should be some sense of closure, either positive or negative, for the main character.

To illustrate these plot parts, we can evaluate a piece of familiar literature, such as George Orwell's Animal Farm. If you've never read the book Animal Farm, go online and read the summary at: http://www.online-literature.com/orwell/animalfarm/

- Complication: Mr. Jones, the farmer, continues to neglect and mistreat the animals. The animals, led by Old Major, hold secret meetings and discuss the possibilities of taking over the farm themselves. Readers can sense the tension building between the humans and the animals.

- Turning Point: The animals are successful at running Mr. Jones off the farm and of taking over. For a brief period, the farm runs smoothly and the animals are content.

- Denouement: Things begin to worsen on the farm. After Napoleon drives Snowball away from the farm, the rules begin to change and the animals begin to be treated more like slaves than equals. One moment of discovery comes when the animals go to the barn and suspect that the rules have been changed.

- Resolution: The animals peer into the farmhouse and discover that the pigs are living like humans. In fact, they can't tell the pigs from the humans.

Of course, the above is a simplified version of the story's plot, but it should illustrate these main components for you.

Setting

Setting is a term referring to the background upon which events take place. That background may include the geographic location, the history of the area, the culture of the surrounding people, etc.

When evaluating literature, setting is often taken for granted. However, it does play an important role in many stories beyond a simple description of the location where the action takes place. For example, the time and geography of Charles Dickens' *A Tale of Two Cities* is vital to the story's plot. Again, if you need to review, here is a link to the summary online: http://www.online-literature.com/dickens/twocities/

The story takes place in two distinct geographic locations: Paris, France and London, England. The plot begins in 1775 and ends in 1793. During that time, the French Revolution begins, which propels the plot of the story.

 Characters

Characters are created by authors to "live" the plot. In most literature, there are at least two main characters: the protagonist and the antagonist. The protagonist is the hero or heroine of the story; he or she is usually the main focus of the plot. The antagonist is the person with whom the protagonist has conflict; he or she is also the one who brings about the protagonist's fall from good fortune.

In William Shakespeare's tragedy *Othello*, Othello is the protagonist and Iago is the antagonist who plots Othello's downfall. Read the summary for Othello included in this study guide.

Most stories also include other characters who help move the plot along or who help readers understand the main characters and their motivations better.

There are also two types of characters: flat and round. Flat characters (often also called stock characters) usually represent one specific quality, such as greed. Their personalities are not fully developed. Round characters, on the other hand, are three-dimensional and have well-developed personalities that allow them to display an array of emotions and reactions. While round characters are usually preferred, especially in the role of protagonist, flat characters can also play important positions in the plot of the story.

Flat characters can also be changed sometimes if they are dynamic. Dynamic characters are those who change in important ways during the course of a work. A good example is Ebenezer Scrooge from Charles Dickens' *A Christmas Carol*. In the beginning of the story, he is a flat character defined mainly by his own greed and lack of compassion for others. By the end of the play, he has become the exact opposite. Read *A Christmas Carol* online: http://www.online-literature.com/dickens/christmascarol/

Not all characters are dynamic, however. Some are static and remain fairly consistent in their attitudes and behaviors throughout the course of a work.

Point of View

Every piece of literature is told from a specific point of view and that point of view affects the story's development dramatically. The chosen point of view is what gives readers their vantage point from which to view the plot and to learn about the characters.

There are two main points of view normally used in literature: first-person and third-person.

A first-person point of view puts the reader inside the mind of one of the characters. Everything that happens is viewed and interpreted through that character. The narrator of the story isn't always the protagonist. In some cases, it's an observer or a minor character.

A third-person point of view provides readers with a less narrow view of the story's developments. There are also two types of third-person points of view: omniscient and limited omniscient. Omniscient narrators can get inside the minds of all of the characters, so that readers can see the story from multiple angles. The limited omniscient narrator may only be able to get inside the minds of a few, or even only one, character.

Third-person narrators can sometimes comment on the developments as they unfold. This method was popular in Jane Austen's works, for example. Other third-person narrators, such as those used by Ernest Hemingway, typically just told the story.

Regardless of the type of point of view used, readers must understand that the narrator is not the author. The narrator is just another character in the work whose view of the action is colored by his or her own personality and experiences just like any other character.

The picaresque novel is usually in first-person. It is a satirical novel which follows a "rascal" or rogue hero of questionably low social status. This hero uses his street smarts in his adventures in his corrupt society.

Mood

Mood is a term that is often difficult to define, but easier to illustrate. The best explanation is that mood refers to the atmosphere of a literary work. The mood usually expresses some type of emotion, such as fear or dread.

A good illustration of mood is found in Edgar Allan Poe's "The Masque of the Red Death." In the story, Prince Prospero has gathered his friends inside his castle to protect them from the ravages of the Red Death. Even though Prospero is throwing a fabulous masquerade party, the mood of the story is never fun or gleeful. Instead, the reader feels a sense of pervasive doom right from the beginning, which only becomes stronger as the story continues. http://www.online-literature.com/poe/36/

Tone

While mood refers to the feeling that is created by the work, tone refers to the author's attitude towards the subject of the work and/or his or her readers. Writers can use a wide variety of tones, including sarcastic, light-hearted, dramatic, passionate, or ironic.

The author's tone shapes the way the readers react to the plot, to the characters, and to the setting. For example, Moliere's play *Tartuffe* clearly includes a satirical and humorous tone. Therefore, the audience views the play in that manner. Read a summary of *Tartuffe* at: http://www.online-literature.com/moliere/tartuffe-or-the-hypocrite/

Theme

Theme refers to the overall main idea or argument proposed by a piece of literature. Unlike the plot, which is usually spelled out for the reader through the actions of the characters, the theme is not always stated and usually requires consideration on the part of the reader.

Most literature contains multiple themes. One theme is primary and is most obvious, but other themes are also present in the work. For example, in *The Grapes of Wrath* by John Steinbeck, one of the most prominent themes is survival. The theme is expressed throughout and is closely tied to the plot. However, other themes, such as the importance of family and social injustice, are also clearly included in the work. Again, another piece of important literature, *Grapes of Wrath* should be read, or at least you should review the summary. http://en.wikipedia.org/wiki/The_Grapes_of_Wrath

Poetry Terminology

While many of the above terms, including theme and character, could also be used in the analysis of poetry, there are some additional terms readers should be familiar with. These terms are primarily focused on the form of the poetry because, unlike in prose, the form of a poem contributes to its meaning.

Meter

The difference between poetry and other forms of literature is meter. All poems must have a recognizable meter. The term itself refers to the arrangement of stressed and unstressed syllables in a line of poetry. The number of syllables is also important.

Discussing meter also requires knowing the term "foot." A foot is a combination of two or more syllables which form a unit of rhythm. The number of feet per line is how readers can analyze a poem's meter. For example, the Iliad was written in hexameter, which means there are six feet per line.

Terms are also used to discuss the pattern of stressed and unstressed syllables in each poetic foot. An iamb is a foot that contains an unstressed and a stressed syllable. A trochee is a foot that contains a stressed and an unstressed syllable. An anapest contains two unstressed and one stressed syllable.

The terms for the number of feet per line and the arrangement of stressed/unstressed syllables can also be combined to label the meter of a poem. One of the most common combinations is iambic pentameter, which is common in English poetry and was popularized in the plays of William Shakespeare. Iambic pentameter means that there are five feet per line and that each of those feet consists of an unstressed syllable followed by a stressed syllable.

Rhyme

Rhyme is another element of poetry. While poems do not have to rhyme, many standard forms do require a specific rhyme scheme.

The term refers to the use of similar ending syllables in lines of poetry. Rhyme, when done well, sounds natural and adds to the rhythm of the poem.

When a poem's rhyme is discussed, it is usually explained by assigning the same letter to each rhyming line of poetry. Take, for example, "Stopping by the Woods on a Snowy Evening" by Robert Frost:

Stopping by the Woods on a Snowy Evening
by Robert Frost

Whose woods these are I think I know. (a)
His house is in the village though; (a)
He will not see me stopping here (b)
To watch his woods fill up with snow. (a)

My little horse must think it queer (b)
To stop without a farmhouse near (b)
Between the woods and frozen lake (c)
The darkest evening of the year. (b)

He gives his harness bells a shake (c)
To ask if there is some mistake. (c)
The only other sound's the sweep (d)
Of easy wind and downy flake. (c)

The woods are lovely, dark and deep, (d)
But I have promises to keep, (d)
And miles to go before I sleep, (d)
And miles to go before I sleep. (d)

The letters beside each line illustrate the poem's rhyme pattern. By using these letters, readers can more clearly see the intentional pattern Frost used in the poem.

Stanza

A stanza refers to the arrangement of the poem's lines. In fact, stanzas are to poems what the paragraph is to a novel. A stanza must contain at least two lines and usually all of the stanzas in a poem should contain the same meter and rhyme, although that's not always the case.

There are different terms to refer to the varying sizes of stanzas found in poetry. Understanding these terms is often useful if you are analyzing or writing a particular poetic form.

- Couplet – 2 lines
- Tercet – 3 lines
- Quatrain – 4 lines
- Quintain – 5 lines
- Sestet – 6 lines
- Septet – 7 lines
- Octave – 8 lines

Epic

An epic is one particular type of poem. Epics are very long narratives (meaning they tell a story) and are written in a more formal style. Epic writers attempt to set their work apart from other popular poetry of the culture by using unusual meters or rhyme schemes. While in Western cultures the most well-known epics are those credited to Homer (*The Iliad* and *The Odyssey*), other cultures have their own epics. *Iliad* http://en.wikipedia.org/wiki/Iliad and *The Odyssey* http://en.wikipedia.org/wiki/Odyssey

Haiku

The haiku is a popular Japanese form of poetry. A haiku consists of three lines. The first and third lines contain 5 syllables and the second contains 7 syllables.

Below is a haiku example written by Matsuo Basho, one of the most famous haiku composers in Japan. In Japanese, this poem follows the correct syllables but because the translation is not exact, it comes out as follows:

An old pond!
A frog jumps in —
the sound of water.

Another example would be:

Wander deeply now
Find knowledge, be determined
Pass test, save money.

Sonnet

The sonnet is another standard poetic form. In fact, there are two versions of the sonnet: the Italian and the English.

The Italian sonnet was popularized by Franceso Petracarca during the 14th century. Italian sonnets consist of one octave followed by a sestet. Italian sonnets also contain a specific rhyme scheme and meter.

English sonnets, often called Shakespearean because William Shakespeare was the most famous sonnet poet, are similar to Italian sonnets in that they have a rigid rhyme and meter scheme to them. In fact, most English sonnets are written in iambic pentameter. The main difference is that an English sonnet consists of three quatrains and a couplet.

Terza Rima

Terza rima is another standard form of poetry. It consists of a series of tercets that are linked together using chain rhyme. Chain rhyme occurs when a rhyme is carried over from one stanza to the next as we saw previously in the "Stopping by the Woods on a Snowy Evening" example. In a terza rima poem, the rhyme scheme would be a-b-a, b-c-b, etc. There is no limit to the number of stanzas that can be included as long as each additional stanza follows the form.

Perhaps the most well-known example of terza rima was Dante's Divine Comedy. John Milton, Lord Byron, and T. S. Eliot also wrote terza rima poems during their careers.

Villanelle

The villanelle form of poetry is popular in the English language. All villanelles consist of five tercets and one quatrain, so they also include 19 lines. The tercets should follow a rhyme scheme of a-b-a while the quatrain's rhyme pattern is a-a-b-a.

While that may seem difficult enough, villanelles also involve repeated lines. For example, the first line of the first tercet becomes the third line of the second, fourth, and sixth stanzas. The poem on the following page, possibly the most well-known villanelle, illustrates this set pattern.

"Do Not Go Gentle Into that Good Night"
by Dylan Thomas

Do not go gentle into that good night,
Old age should burn and rave at close of day;
Rage, rage against the dying of the light.

Though wise men at their end know dark is right,
Because their words had forked no lightning they
Do not go gentle into that good night.

Good men, the last wave by, crying how bright
Their frail deeds might have danced in a green bay,
Rage, rage against the dying of the light.

Wild men who caught and sang the sun in flight,
And learn, too late, they grieved it on its way,
Do not go gentle into that good night.

Grave men, near death, who see with blinding sight
Blind eyes could blaze like meteors and be gay,
Rage, rage against the dying of the light.

And you, my father, there on the sad height,
Curse, bless, me now with your fierce tears, I pray.
Do not go gentle into that good night.
Rage, rage against the dying of the light.

Rhyme Royal

Geoffrey Chaucer created the rhyme royal form of poetry in the 14th century. Rhyme royal poems include seven lines (written as either a quatrain and a tercet or a tercet followed by two couplets) written in iambic pentameter. The poems must also follow an exact rhyme scheme: a-b-a-b-b-c-c. Multiple units of seven lines can be linked together to form longer narratives as well. Chaucer used rhyme royal in many of his poems and in a few of the stories in the Canterbury Tales.

Sestina

One of the more complex poetry forms in the English language is the sestina. Sestinas consist of 39 lines, which are broken down into six sestets and one tercet. Sestinas are normally written in iambic pentameter.

The challenging part of a sestina is that the same six words must be reused at the end of the lines of every stanza, but in a very specific pattern. The six words are also included in the concluding tercet in a prescribed manner as well. Below is an example which illustrates this pattern:

Sestina
by Dante Alighieri

I have come, alas, to the great circle of shadow,
to the short day and to the whitening hills,
when the colour is all lost from the grass,
though my desire will not lose its green,
so rooted is it in this hardest stone,
that speaks and feels as though it were a woman.

And likewise this heaven-born woman
stays frozen, like the snow in shadow,
and is unmoved, or moved like a stone,
by the sweet season that warms all the hills,
and makes them alter from pure white to green,
so as to clothe them with the flowers and grass.

When her head wears a crown of grass
she draws the mind from any other woman,
because she blends her gold hair with the green
so well that Amor lingers in their shadow,
he who fastens me in these low hills,
more certainly than lime fastens stone.

Her beauty has more virtue than rare stone.
The wound she gives cannot be healed with grass,
since I have travelled, through the plains and hills,
to find my release from such a woman,
yet from her light had never a shadow
thrown on me, by hill, wall, or leaves' green.

I have seen her walk all dressed in green,
so formed she would have sparked love in a stone,
that love I bear for her very shadow,
so that I wished her, in those fields of grass,
as much in love as ever yet was woman,
closed around by all the highest hills.

The rivers will flow upwards to the hills
before this wood, that is so soft and green,
takes fire, as might ever lovely woman,
for me, who would choose to sleep on stone,
all my life, and go eating grass,
only to gaze at where her clothes cast shadow.

Whenever the hills cast blackest shadow,
with her sweet green, the lovely woman
hides it, as a man hides stone in grass.

Blank Verse

Unlike many forms of poetry, blank verse does not have as many restrictions. The distinguishing factor for blank verse poetry is that it has a set meter (usually iambic pentameter) but does not rhyme.

Christopher Marlowe used blank verse often in his work Dr. Faustus. William Shakespeare and John Keats also used blank verse regularly in their poems. However, one of the most effective and well-known examples of blank verse was John Milton's *Paradise Lost*. The passage below illustrates Milton's use of this particular form:

Into what Pit thou seest
From what highth fal'n, so much the stronger provd
He with his Thunder: and till then who knew
The force of those dire Arms? yet not for those
Nor what the Potent Victor in his rage
Can else inflict do I repent or change,
Though chang'd in outward lustre; that fixt mind
And high disdain, from sence of injur'd merit,
That with the mightiest rais'd me to contend,
And to the fierce contention brought along
Innumerable force of Spirits arm'd

That durst dislike his reign, and me preferring,
His utmost power with adverse power oppos'd
In dubious Battel on the Plains of Heav'n,
And shook his throne. What though the field be lost?
All is not lost; the unconquerable Will,
And study of revenge, immortal hate,
And courage never to submit or yield:

Free Verse

Free verse is a style of poetry that has no set qualifications. There is no set pattern of stanzas, no limits on the number of lines, and no specific meter. Rhyme schemes are also optional in free verse poetry.

There is a debate among poets about the merits of free verse. Robert Frost once compared the practice of writing free verse to "playing tennis without a net." Other poets, such as Walt Whitman and Ezra Pound, found free verse to be a strong channel of expression and felt it was equal to the most restrictive forms.

Other Important Terms

While we've already discussed terms related to the study of literature and poetry, there are some terms which are commonly used in the analysis of both. Many of these terms represent figures of speech (expressions designed intentionally to create a certain effect on the audience) and assist readers in more fully understanding a work of prose or of poetry.

Allegory

An allegory is a method of story-telling which has two distinct levels of meaning. On the one hand, the story can be interpreted literally. For example, *Animal Farm* can be a story about pigs leading a revolt against humans on a farm. However, allegories also include a much deeper meaning. In *Animal Farm*, the pigs revolt and the consequences represent the Communist Revolution and its ramifications in Russia. Other well-known allegoric works include John Bunyan's *Pilgrim's Progress* and Dante Alighieri's *The Divine Comedy*.

Alliteration

Alliteration is a stylistic method of creating a sense of rhythm and of attracting attention to specific passages in poetry and in prose. With alliteration, the initial sounds of close words are the same. The following lines from Dylan Thomas's "Fern Hill" illustrate alliteration: "I should hear him fly with the high fields / And wake to the farm forever fled from the childless land."

Assonance and consonance are similar methods. Assonance refers to the repetition of vowel sounds while consonance refers to the repetition of consonant sounds. Both differ from alliteration because the repeated sounds do not have to be at the beginning of the words.

Allusion

Allusions are references to events, people, places, or ideas that are commonly known. Allusions can come from history, literature, movies, music, or any other shared part of culture. The only pre-requisite for an allusion is that it be recognizable by the majority of educated readers. Unfamiliar allusions fail to make their point because readers don't recognize them.

Antithesis

Another common stylistic device is the antithesis. Antithesis combines two ideas that seem contradictory in order to make a larger point. Franklin D. Roosevelt's first inaugural address in 1933 contained one of the most well-known examples of antithesis: "The only thing we have to fear is fear itself."

Hyperbole

Hyperbole is a figure of speech. It's an exaggeration used to emphasize a point. The two following lines from Ralph Waldo Emerson's "The Concord Hymn" illustrate hyperbole: "Here once the embattled farmers stood / And fired the shot heard round the world."

Imagery

In prose and poetry, imagery is a critical component because it makes the events come to life in the mind of the reader. Imagery refers to words and figures of speech which are used to create a picture of events, people, or settings in literature. The final stanza of Edgar Allan Poe's "The Raven" is a good example of effective imagery:

And the raven, never flitting, still is sitting, still is sitting
On the pallid bust of Pallas just above my chamber door;
And his eyes have all the seeming of a demon's that is dreaming,
And the lamp-light o'er him streaming throws his shadow on the floor;
And my soul from out that shadow that lies floating on the floor
Shall be lifted - nevermore!

Irony

Irony is a stylistic device involving different interpretations of actions and words in literature. Essentially, what is being said or done is not what it seems to be. One type of irony – tragic irony – involves the audience or reader by allowing them to recognize the tragic fate of the protagonist before he or she experiences it.

One of the best examples of tragic irony is from the Greek play *Oedipus the King* by Sophocles. In the play, Oedipus has fled from his family because of a prophecy that said he would murder his father and marry his mother. During his journey, he is made king and marries the queen, whose former husband was killed. Because the killer of the past king was not punished, the city is made to suffer and Oedipus promises to track down the killer and ensure that justice is done. It turns out that he was the killer, the former king was his father, and his current wife was his mother. http://en.wikipedia.org/wiki/Oedipus

Metaphor/Simile

Two of the most common figures of speech are metaphors and similes. These are commonly used to assist in the creation of vivid imagery in both prose and poetry.

A simile is a comparison between two unlike things using the words "like" or "as." A metaphor is also a comparison between two unlike things but without the words "like" or "as."

Similes are also short. Metaphors can be brief, or they can be extended.

 # Onomatopoeia

This figure of speech uses a specific word that captures or imitates the sound it is being used to describe. For example, the word "buzz" is used to describe the buzzing sound made by bees. The word imitates that sound. "Plop" and "tick tock" are two other examples of onomatopoeia.

 # Style

The idea of a writer's style is something that is often discussed but rarely defined. Writing style encompasses many elements and it is the combination of these elements that creates a uniqueness for each author.

These elements include word choice, subject matter, point of view, characterization, setting, tone, theme, etc. Each writer must work at refining his or her own style in order to set them apart from other writers.

Symbolism

Understanding symbolism is an important part of deciphering the meaning and significance of prose and poetry. The idea is that objects, people, settings, or ideas in a story may have two meanings: a literal one and a symbolic one. In Edgar Allan Poe's "The Raven," for example, the bird is both literally a raven and a symbol of death and loss. The bird's cryptic promise to leave him "nevermore" symbolizes the narrator's feelings that he will never get over the pain or memory of his love's death.

Another example of symbolism is the green light in F. Scott Fitzgerald's *The Great Gatsby*. The green light symbolizes all of the things Gatsby is yearning for in the novel, specifically Daisy. http://en.wikipedia.org/wiki/The_great_gatsby

Personification

This common figure of speech allows writers to give animals or other inanimate objects human qualities. Below are a few lines from a poem called "Mirror" by Sylvia Plath that illustrates personification by attributing human qualities to a mirror:

I am silver and exact. I have no preconceptions.
What ever you see I swallow immediately
Just as it is, unmisted by love or dislike.
I am not cruel, only truthful---
The eye of a little god, four-cornered.

 # Literary Periods

Literature has gone through a number of periods or phases since its beginnings. Each of these phases includes an emphasis on different themes and techniques by the writers of the time. Their works are influenced by the historic and cultural settings around them; therefore, studying the literature of these different periods can help readers not only gain more insight into the works themselves but also into the times in which they were written.

Although literature has a long history of its own and comes from every corner of the globe, our focus will be on literature from the Medieval period to the modern era and on works from the Western world.

 # Mythology - Prometheus

Prometheus was a Greek Titan known for his trickery and cunning. After the war between the Titans and the Gods he was not punished because he sided with the Gods and used his cunning to help them. He was respected as being a helper of mankind. Due to a trick of Prometheus, the precedent was set that fat and bones, rather than the more useful and preferable meat, should be sacrificed to the gods. Zeus was angered by the trickery of Prometheus and withheld fire from mankind.

However, Prometheus once again helped mankind by stealing some fire and introducing it to mortals. Angered even further, Zeus had Pandora created and she released all forms of temptation upon mankind. Prometheus was further punished by Zeus, who sentenced him to be tied up and have his liver eaten each day by a giant eagle, only to have it regrow that night. The seemingly eternal punishment was not ended until Hercules was one day allowed to slay the eagle as a show of bravery and strength.

Medieval Period

The Medieval Period of literature stretches from around the fall of the Roman Empire in 476 A.D to about the 15th century (the start of the Renaissance in Italy). Because much of what had been left behind by the Greeks and the Romans had been lost, the Medieval Period is not simply an extension of those Western teachings and writing styles.

Religion dominated most of literature during this time because of the strength of the Catholic Church. Writers, such as Thomas Aquinas, wrote about religious teachings and ethics. Allegoric plays, such as *Everyman*, were the only type of theater allowed by the Church. These plays were used to re-emphasize Biblical teachings and are often referred to as Morality Plays.

Despite the prevalence of religious-based literature, some secular works also appeared. Troubadours during the 11th century traveled around and composed poems about "courtly love" to the wives and daughters of knights who were away serving their lords. Epic poems, such as those written by Homer, were also popular in certain cultures. Two of the most well-known of these epics are *Beowulf* and *The Song of Roland*. http://en.wikipedia.org/wiki/Beowolf and http://en.wikipedia.org/wiki/The_Song_of_Roland

While the vast majority of Medieval writers and poets were male, some women were also able to gain attention through their writings as well. Hildegard of Bingen and Christine de Pizan wrote stories and other works that provide a female-view of religion and society during the time period.

The fabliaux was a style of writing initially popularized in France in the 12th century, but which spread in small measure to England and other parts of Europe. The fabliaux were sarcastic, cynical, and comic stories, usually in poetic verse, which typically focused on topics such as adultery and other social obscenities. Some of the most well-known fabliaux are found in Chaucer's *Canterbury Tales*, including the *Miller's Tale* and the *Reeve's Tale*.

Among the most well-known writings of the Medieval Period are the following:

• *The Book of the City of Ladies* by Christine de Pizan

• *Consolation of Philosophy* by Boethius

- *The Canterbury Tales* by Geoffrey Chaucer

- *Decameron* by Giovanni Boccaccio

- *The Divine Comedy* by Dante Alighieri

- *Revelations of Divine Love* by Julian of Norwich

- *Scivias* by Hildegard of Bingen

- *Summar Theologica* by Thomas Aquinas

- *Sir Gawain and the Green Knight* by Gawain-poet (anonymous)

- *Le Morte d'Arthur* by Sir Thomas Malory

Memorize these titles and authors!

King Arthur

The legends surrounding King Arthur are some of the most penetrating legends to emerge from French and British medieval cultures. Not only did the legends dominate literature of the time, but their themes, plots, and characters find their way into literature today. The legends begin with Uther Pendragon, the king, who secretly fathers a son Arthur. However, because of trouble within the kingdom, Arthur is given to the wizard Merlin to raise him. When Uther passes away the kingdom is in turmoil because he has left no male heirs. Merlin sets a sword in stone and announces that whoever can pull the sword free is the rightful king.

Despite intense efforts to free the sword, all fail at the task. The young Arthur is sent in search of a sword for his cousin and accidentally happens across the sword in the stone. He succeeds in pulling it free, and is named the new king. However, he still must win the loyalty of the court and the knights. Through many acts of bravery, impressive shows of skill, and the help of Merlin, Arthur is able to win the admiration and loyalty of the knights, and he successfully fights off a Saxon invasion. The stories of King Arthur and his legendary Knights of the Round Table are stories of fantastic bravery and courage. Many of them center on the search for the Holy Grail from which Jesus Christ was said to have drunk. Eventually Arthur is wounded in battle and sent to the mysterious Isle of Avalon for healing. According to legend, he will one day return to lead Britain through its most troubling time. This has earned him the title of "now and future king."

Death Be Not Proud

Death Be Not Proud (also known as Sonnet X) is the most famous poem of John Donne. The author uses personification of death to offer a criticism of it and express a lack of fear. Rather than cowering in the face of death, Donne defies the finality of death by claiming that death is truly slave to men – whether by war, stupidity or some other cause. Further, Donne concludes the sonnet with a statement that death itself will die. Donne's Christian faith in a future resurrection frees him from fear of death, which he sees as only temporary.

Piers Plowman

Piers Plowman, sometimes known as *The Vision of Piers Plowman,* is a medieval poem attributed to William Langland sometime in the late 14th century. It is considered to be one of the most difficult medieval texts because it was so frequently revised by the author that every surviving copy is slightly different. The poem is highly allegorical and written in alliterative verse. It tells the story of a character named Will who has a series of visions through which he searches for Truth (a figurative person symbolic of ultimate truth in the real world). Throughout his dream-visions, Will encounters characters such as False, Mercy, Conscience, Justice, Peace, Study, Clergy, Scripture, and the Holy Church among others.

His interactions with the various characters teach social and spiritual principles as he continues his search for Truth. Along the way Will is also guided by a plowman named Piers who becomes symbolic of Christ. The poem details the events of the crucifixion, and Will sees that only Christ can reclaim the souls that the Devil has taken. As a spiritual commentary, the poem ultimately identifies works and grace as the two pillars which salvation rests upon.

Renaissance Period

Before the start of the 16th century, changes were beginning to take place throughout Europe. Three of those changes signaled the start of a new period in literature and culture which is now known as the Renaissance. Johann Gutenberg's development of the printing press allowed books and other materials to be more easily distributed and encouraged more people to learn how to read. Another change was that Europe opened trade routes with both China and India. This exposure to different cultures opened their minds and caused people to move away from the Medieval focus on Christianity.

The Renaissance brought about a renewed interest in learning and in improving the individual. The Renaissance also focused on logic and rational thought.

English playwrights such as William Shakespeare and Christopher Marlowe appreciated a renewed appreciation for drama that had been missing from the Medieval period. Philosophers, such as Thomas More and Francis Bacon, also became popular during the Renaissance.

Poets like Shakespeare and Franceso Petrach were also crafting new styles that still influence modern poetry. Petrach, in fact, popularized the Italian sonnet. During the latter part of the Renaissance, a trend in metaphysical poetry began. These poets, such as John Donne, used their works to try and understand their faith and their environment instead of simply accepting answers provided by religious teachings.

The novel also became an important literary development. *Don Quixote* by Miguel Cervantes is considered the first European novel, although some credit *Le Morte d'Arthur* by Sir Thomas Malory as a precursor to the form.

Among the most well-known writings of the Renaissance Period are the following:

- *Hamlet, Romeo and Juliet*, and other plays by William Shakespeare

- *Doctor Faustus* by Christopher Marlowe

- *Utopia* by Sir Thomas More

- *The Alchemist* by Ben Jonson

- *Don Quixote* by Miguel Cervantes

- *Essays* by Francis Bacon

- *The Prince* by Niccolo Machiavelli

- *Songs and Sonnets* by John Donne

- "To His Coy Mistress" by Andrew Marvell

- *Tartuffe* by Moliere

- *The Faerie Queen* by Edmund Spenser

Hamlet

As *Hamlet* begins, the royal family of Denmark is in disarray. The King of Denmark recently died and now his brother Claudius married the widowed Queen Gertrude, thus making him the new king. With Denmark under new rule, the country faces an impending invasion from a young man named Fortinbras whose father was murdered by Hamlet's father. Fortinbras wants to reclaim the land that was taken by Hamlet's father, thus he plans to invade Denmark. King Claudius attempts to stop the upcoming invasion by writing to Fortinbras' uncle, the King of Norway.

Prince Hamlet is tormented by his father's death and by his mother's hasty decision to remarry. When his father's ghost visits Hamlet and tells him that Claudius poisoned him, he instructs Hamlet to get revenge on Claudius but to let his mother live in peace. As his father's ghost departs, Hamlet vows to remember his father's words and to avenge his untimely death. When Marcellus, one of the night watchmen, and Horatio, Hamlet's dear friend, ask Hamlet what the ghost said, Hamlet refuses to answer. His father's ghost reappears and makes the men promise not to divulge any of the events they have seen. This promise later guides the action of the play, as the only two people who understand Hamlet's oddities are unable to vouch for his sanity.

Meanwhile, Hamlet is in love with a young woman named Ophelia. Her brother Laertes and her father Polonius instruct her to avoid Hamlet and his attempts to woo her. As an obedient daughter and sister, Ophelia obeys her family's commands. Shortly after their conversation, Laertes leaves to continue his education in Paris. Soon after, Hamlet begins to demonstrate signs of insanity that stem from his interaction with his father's ghost. Polonius thinks that Hamlet is acting mad because he is love sick over Ophelia's decision to shun him. After Hamlet approaches Ophelia under the guise of a mad man, Ophelia cannot help but agree and she reports Hamlet's behavior to King Claudius.

As Hamlet's sanity continues to decline, King Claudius and Queen Gertrude try to determine the cause of Hamlet's mental transformation. Queen Gertrude believes that Hamlet is distraught over his father's death and over his mother's decision to remarry so quickly. In an attempt to help Hamlet, King Claudius and Queen Gertrude send for Hamlet's lifelong friends Guildenstern and Rosencrantz to visit. It does not take long for readers to realize that King Claudius has an ulterior motive because he tells Polonius that he wants Hamlet to leave for England with his friends.

When Guildenstern and Rosencrantz meet with Hamlet, they attempt to cheer him up by telling him that a traveling group of actors will perform a play for the royal court. Hamlet tells his friends that he knows they are truly there to cure his madness, but he confesses that he is not truly mad. While Hamlet speaks with his friends, Polonius enters to tell him that the acting troupe has arrived. Hamlet asks the actors if they could put on an altered version of *The Murder of Gonzago* to which Hamlet will supply the additional lines. Since Hamlet wants to be sure that his father's ghost was a true apparition and not a devil in disguise, he believes that this play will reveal the truth.

If King Claudius appears guilty when he watches the play the next night, Hamlet will know that he truly is a murderer. However, if King Claudius is unaffected by the altered version of the play, Hamlet will know that his father's ghost is the villain.

Soon after Hamlet plots to learn the truth, the rest of the characters in the play plot to understand Hamlet's source of madness. With the exception of King Claudius and Polonius who hide themselves, the group exits the room while Ophelia pretends to read from a book of prayers. At this point, Hamlet enters the room and recites his infamous "To be or not to be" speech. He denounces all of the former affection that he showed Ophelia and denounces the very concept of marriage. After he states that all marriages will remain the same except for one, he vacates the area. King Claudius is immediately suspicious and reiterates his plans to send Hamlet to England.

When it is time for the play, Hamlet is pleased to see that his mother and King Claudius are in the audience. Hamlet asks Horatio to watch King Claudius to gauge his reaction to the night's performance. This play within a play is remarkably similar to Hamlet's personal tale. It involves a king who is poisoned in the ear and a queen who quickly marries the murderer. King Claudius asks Hamlet if this play is meant to be offensive and Hamlet responds that the play should not offend anybody who has a clear conscience. At the point in the play when the original king is murdered, King Claudius rapidly leaves the room. Hamlet and Horatio assume that this action proves that the ghost spoke the truth.

After the play, Guildenstern and Rosencrantz again try to make Hamlet reveal the reason for his apparent madness and they advise him to visit his mother. Hamlet is aware that they are on King Claudius' side and he tells his friends not to "play upon" him. When Polonius enters and asks Hamlet to visit Queen Gertrude, Hamlet leaves to go to her chambers. As he is on his way to visit his mother, Hamlet sees King Claudius praying. Unaware that Claudius is lamenting over murdering his own brother and thus unable to cleanse himself in prayer, Hamlet decides that he cannot kill King Claudius while he prays. To do so would mean that King Claudius might go to Heaven and that would defeat the very purpose of Hamlet's revenge.

When Hamlet enters Queen Gertrude's chambers, he does not realize that Polonius is hiding behind the arras so that he can overhear the conversation. As Hamlet chastises his mother for betraying her first husband, he hears a sound from behind the arras. Assuming that King Claudius is the eavesdropper, Hamlet jabs his sword through the curtain and murders Polonius. Soon after, the ghost of Hamlet's father enters the room again, but only Hamlet can see him. Queen Gertrude is frightened by Hamlet's apparent conversation with himself. However, she quickly realizes the error of her hasty and incestuous marriage and promises not to reveal Hamlet's sanity to anyone.

Queen Gertrude keeps her promise and tells King Claudius that Hamlet murdered Polonius and that he weeps for his murderous action. King Claudius is not impressed with this proof of Hamlet's madness and he reminds his wife that Hamlet will leave for England at daybreak. Rosencrantz and Guildenstern try to get Hamlet to tell them where he hid Polonius' body, but Hamlet will not reveal the hiding place. When his supposed friends bring him to see King Claudius, Hamlet remains coy about Polonius' resting place. King Claudius tells Hamlet that he will go to England with his friends for his own safety. Of course, the king does not mention that Hamlet is set to die when he arrives. Thankfully, Hamlet soon manages to return to Denmark where he meets with Horatio.

Meanwhile, Ophelia's sanity has greatly diminished since her father died and Hamlet left for England. Laertes quickly returns from Paris and promises to avenge his father's murder. As part of his new master plan to be rid of his nephew/stepson, King Claudius arranges a duel between Laertes and Hamlet, in which Laertes is supposed to stab Hamlet with a poisoned sword tip. On the off chance that the poisoned sword tip does not kill him, King Claudius plans to poison Hamlet's drink which he will undoubtedly need during the duel. Laertes agrees to this plan, but his motivation quickly diminishes when a servant enters the room to say that Ophelia drowned while she was hanging flowers on a tree by a river.

Due to Ophelia's mental state, nobody knows whether her death was an accident or a suicide. Since she is a gentlewoman, they decide that she can have a semi-Christian burial. There will not be any songs or sacraments, but her body can be properly buried. Hamlet happens to wander to the grave site at which point he encounters Laertes. The two begin to fight, but the fight is stopped because King Claudius wants to proceed with the original plan.

In the final act of the play, Hamlet reveals to Horatio that he knew that Guildenstern and Rosencrantz carried a letter which would have doomed Hamlet to his death. To retaliate, he rewrote the letters so that his supposed friends will be the ones to die. Soon after, Hamlet receives a formal request asking him to engage in a duel with Laertes. King Claudius claims that he bet on Hamlet's victory and Hamlet agrees to participate in the duel.

During the battle, Queen Gertrude heeds her husband's advice and drinks from the poisoned cup. Hamlet and Laertes accidentally switch swords during the duel and both men injure one another. Queen Gertrude realizes that she has been poisoned and she dies. Laertes reveals that both he and Hamlet are also doomed because King Claudius poisoned the cup and the sword that injured both men. Hamlet forces King Claudius to drink the rest of the poison, thus seeking his revenge. With the truth exposed, Hamlet and Laertes reconcile their differences right before Laertes dies. At that moment, Fortinbras returns and Hamlet names him as the next King of Denmark. After his decree, Hamlet dies and Fortinbras declares that Hamlet will be buried as a good ruler because he was "a good soldier."

 Macbeth

This tragedy begins with a sinister tone as the Weird Sisters – also known as the three witches – prophesize the events that are to come. They state that the civil war in Scotland will quickly end and that they will soon meet with the hero Macbeth. With their line, "Fear is foul and foul is fair," the Weird Sisters end the first scene with the foreshadowing that evil is sure to come.

Meanwhile, King Duncan is happy to learn that Macbeth successfully defeated Macdonwald and ended the war. He also learns that the Thane of Cawdor betrayed him, at which point he executes the previous Thane and proclaims that virtuous Macbeth will be the new Thane of Cawdor.

When Macbeth and his friend Banquo encounter the Weird Sisters, they are quite surprised by the prophecies they hear. The Sisters tell the men that Macbeth will become the Thane of Cawdor and eventually the King. Banquo asks what will become of him and the Sisters tell him that he will never be a king but his sons will be. After they pique Macbeth's self-interest, the Sisters disappear. Shortly after, Macbeth learns that the first part of the prophecy has come true; he is now the Thane of Cawdor. Once Macbeth sees the truth in the Sisters' words, he cannot help but forget their evil nature. His lust for power begins to grow and he wants nothing more than to become king.

Now that royalty is on Macbeth's mind, he is eager to become king as quickly as possible. His eagerness proves to be a problem when King Duncan decrees that his son Malcolm is the heir to the crown. Macbeth discusses his plight with Lady Macbeth and she encourages him to do whatever he must to become the king. Soon after, King Duncan arrives at their home and Lady Macbeth instructs her husband to be courteous to their guest – for now. Though Macbeth wants nothing more than to become king, he feels a tremendous amount of guilt for his plot to kill his cousin and king. Lady Macbeth accuses Macbeth of being a coward and insists that he carry out his plan. At this point, she wants to be queen as much as he wants to be king, so she attempts to counteract Macbeth's conscience with their mutual lust for power and royalty.

That night, Macbeth lurks in the hallway and prepares to kill King Duncan. His conscience still weighs heavy on him and it is not until a dagger appears before him that he prepares to act. When he hears Lady Macbeth ring her bell, Macbeth stabs the king to death. In a panic, he flees from the room with the bloodied weapon in his hands. Lady Macbeth eagerly awaits her husband's return and she is relieved that he carried out their plan. She urges him to return the dagger to the murder scene, but Macbeth cannot bring himself to go back into that room. To ensure that their plan is successful, Lady Macbeth returns the daggers and stains her hands with the blood.

Soon after, the murder is discovered and Macbeth claims that he saw the servants murder the king and that he could not help but kill them in retaliation. King Duncan's sons are terrified after their father is murdered and they flee the country to save themselves. With their absence, the second part of the Weird Sisters' prophecy comes true and Macbeth becomes the king.

Now that the Sisters' prophecies about Macbeth have been fulfilled, Banquo begins to wonder about his sons and how they fit into prophecy. Banquo still tries to act as Macbeth's friend, but he suspects that Macbeth may have killed Duncan to ensure his role as king. Macbeth is just as suspicious of Banquo and he fears that his friend's sons will replace him as king. Without telling his wife of his plans, Macbeth pays two men to kill Banquo and his son Fleance while they are horse riding for the day. The murderers successfully slay Banquo, but Fleance gets away. When Macbeth hears of the events that transpired, he is happy to know that Banquo is dead and that he will not be able to breed any more potential heirs to the throne. He promises to take care of Fleance at a later time.

Meanwhile, a fourth witch named Hecate is introduced to the story. She is upset that the Weird Sisters did not consult her before they began to unravel Macbeth's life, but she vows to help them finish what they started. While he is at a banquet, Macbeth sees Banquo's ghost. He engages in horrified conversation with the apparition and the other guests who cannot see the ghost wonder what is wrong with Macbeth. When the ghost finally disappears, Macbeth determines that he must speak with the Weird Sisters again to understand what is happening.

When Macbeth visits the witches, they show him three apparitions that proclaim three more prophecies. The first apparition tells Macbeth that he should be careful of Macduff, a Scottish nobleman. The second apparition tells Macbeth that he cannot be harmed by any man who was born of a woman. The final apparition states that Macbeth will remain in power until Birnam marches to Dunsinane. As a final prophecy, Macbeth sees an image of a long line of kings. The last king looks at himself in the mirror and Macbeth sees that the final king appears to be Banquo. With his new knowledge, Macbeth has Macduff's family killed and he travels to England to kill Macduff himself. When Macduff learns that his family has been slain, he promises to help Malcolm put a stop to Macbeth.

While Macbeth is consumed in his quest to maintain his power, Lady Macbeth slowly loses her mind. Her conscience has finally set in and she cannot stop thinking about what she and her husband have done. Her attendant is so shocked by the things that Lady Macbeth says in her sleep that she makes the doctor hear the mad woman's words himself. Macbeth does not realize the severity of his wife's condition. As she wanders around trying to scrub the imaginary blood from her hands, Macbeth can only think of his own position. When Macbeth receives word that his wife is dead, he is not even concerned enough to ask what happened to her. He just continues on his quest to keep the throne.

At this point, the opposing army camouflages themselves by carrying branches from Birnam Wood as they prepare to battle Macbeth. When Macbeth sees the third part of the Sisters' prophecy come true, he becomes alarmed. However, he is still confident that he cannot be killed by any man born of woman, so he is not too concerned. While Macbeth fights Macduff, Macbeth informs his adversary that he cannot be killed because every man is born of a woman. Macduff retaliates by saying that he was not technically born of a woman because he was surgically taken out of his mother's womb. With his confidence gone, Macbeth is quickly killed by Macduff. Malcolm is then proclaimed as the rightful King of Scotland, and he promises to make his country the peaceful place that it was before the story of Macbeth and the Weird Sisters.

 Othello

The action in *Othello* begins after Othello, the Moor of Venice, elopes with his beloved Desdemona. Othello's ensign Iago approaches one of Desdemona's failed suitors named Roderigo and explains how much he hates Othello. Iago feels that he should have been promoted to Othello's lieutenant, but Othello gave that position to a man named Michael Cassio. The enraged Iago is furious that Othello gave him the more demeaning position of ensign. Foreshadowing the evil that lies within the ensign, Iago persuades the failed suitor Roderigo to join his side. The two plotting men wake up Desdemona's father Brabantio to tell him of his daughter's secret marriage.

Brabantio is angry with his daughter's decision and Iago uses that anger to begin his duplicitous plot against Othello. Iago tells Othello how angry Brabantio was and claims that he had to restrain himself from attacking Brabantio for insulting Othello. The gentle Othello tells Iago that there is no need to worry because he truly loves Desdemona and his intentions are noble. As Othello explains his love, he is summonsed to see the Duke of Venice in regards to an upcoming military trip to Cyprus. At that moment, Brabantio,

Roderigo, and some officers try to attack Othello for tricking Desdemona into loving him. Othello again asserts that his love is true and together the men leave to attend the military conference.

At the conference, the men learn that Cyprus is in danger of being attacked by a Turkish fleet. Brabantio again accuses Othello of tricking Desdemona into loving him, but Desdemona interjects that she loves her husband and that she must choose her husband over her father as her mother once chose Brabantio over her father. Desdemona's testimony ends the argument over her marriage and the conference resumes its business. Othello will go to Cyprus to defend the land. Iago and his wife Emilia will ensure that Desdemona arrives in Cyprus safely. After the conference ends, Iago reveals his ulterior motives to the audience and decides that he will get his revenge by convincing Othello that Desdemona is having an affair with Michael Cassio.

The journey to Cyprus turns out to be unnecessary as the Turkish fleet is destroyed by a severe storm. All of the main characters safely arrive to Cyprus and are overjoyed to see that the war is over. When Iago notices how polite Cassio is to Desdemona, he realizes how easy his plan will be. Iago deceivingly tells Roderigo that Desdemona will not want to be with Othello forever. In fact, she is already in love with Cassio. This is a lie, but Roderigo loves Desdemona so he is willing to listen. Iago convinces Roderigo to pick a fight with Cassio so that Othello will have no choice but to remove Cassio from his ranks. With Desdemona's potential love on his mind, Roderigo agrees with Iago's plan.

Later that night, the characters celebrate a feast in honor of Othello and Desdemona's marriage. Iago lies to Cassio and tells him that he is relieved of his duty for the night, at which point Iago makes sure to get Cassio drunk. Iago then tells Roderigo to attack Cassio, which leads to a scuffle. When Othello sees Cassio in his drunken and violent state, he strips him of his title. Ever deceitful, Iago tells Cassio that Desdemona will pity his situation and that he should seek her help in regaining his title. Cassio asks for Desdemona's help and she agrees to speak to her husband on Cassio's behalf.

Iago plants the seed of doubt in Othello's mind when he says that Desdemona cannot be trusted. Torn between his love for Desdemona and his trust in Iago's words, Othello does not know what to think. He tells Iago that he will need solid proof of Desdemona's infidelity before he can take action. That proof comes later when Desdemona wipes Othello's brow with her handkerchief. He knocks the piece of cloth from her hand and Emilia picks it up. Iago takes the handkerchief from his wife and later tells Othello that he saw Cassio wiping his face with Desdemona's handkerchief. This serves as proof of his wife's infidelity and Othello promises to get revenge on Cassio.

Othello asks Desdemona to use the handkerchief that he gave her and she tells him that she misplaced it. This confirms Othello's suspicions and he scolds Desdemona for losing his mother's handkerchief. Soon after, Cassio enters the room and asks Desdemona to speak to Othello about him. Desdemona tells Cassio that Othello is behaving strangely and that he should wait until Othello is in a better mood.

A bit later, Cassio's mistress Bianca enters his chambers and asks why he has not been spending much time with her lately. He tells her that things have been hectic and he gives her the handkerchief that Iago hid in his room. Bianca is convinced that he got the handkerchief from another woman. Cassio swears that he did not get it from another woman and he asks Bianca to copy the design to make a similar handkerchief. What Cassio does not realize is that his action places him even deeper into Iago's wicked plan.

Iago continues to fill Othello's mind with thoughts of infidelity and suggests that Othello should eavesdrop while Iago talks with Cassio. While Iago talks to Cassio about Bianca, Othello mistakenly thinks they are talking about Desdemona. When Bianca enters the scene and throws the handkerchief at Cassio, Othello is certain that Desdemona is guilty. Unaware that Iago has orchestrated this entire scheme, Othello vows to kill his wife.

Meanwhile, Roderigo grows weary waiting for his chance with Desdemona. Iago advises him to kill Cassio to expedite Desdemona's love for him. Roderigo takes his advice and starts a fight with Cassio. Roderigo gets wounded and Iago stabs Cassio to prove his supposed loyalty to Othello. Before Roderigo can tell anybody what really happened, Iago kills him.

Othello sits in Desdemona's chambers and thinks about his plight while she sleeps. He says "I know not where is that Promethean heat - That can thy light relume." This means that he knows that if he kills her, it will be final. Unfortunately, his decision is made and when his wife awakens, he tells her that she must pray before she dies. Othello then suffocates his beloved wife, at which point Emilia enters and witnesses what he has done. Othello tells her of Desdemona's infidelity and of the proof of the handkerchief. Emilia tells Othello that Iago had the handkerchief and proves Iago's guilt. When Iago enters the room, he kills his wife. Othello attempts to kill Iago, but Iago is arrested. Refusing to explain his actions, Iago leaves Othello to wonder what happened. In a fit of despair, Othello stabs himself and kisses his wife one final time before he dies.

Romeo and Juliet

As the prologue states, *Romeo and Juliet* is the story of two influential families (the Capulets and the Montagues) who have engaged in a familial feud for quite some time. Both of these families reside in the city of Verona and both families hold equal societal statuses. Since these "two households both alike in dignity" cannot end their feud in a dignified manner, they continue to fight on the streets of Verona. The problem escalates further when Romeo, the only Montague son, falls in love with Juliet, the only Capulet daughter. Since these young lovers are "star-cross'd," their relationship is ultimately destined to fail. Thus Shakespeare ends his prologue by proclaiming that the mismatched lovers, their familial feud, and their inevitable deaths will be the focal points of the story.

The play begins when the Capulets and the Montagues engage in a battle of wits which eventually escalates to a physical battle. When the brawl ends, the Prince proclaims that if these two families get in another public fight, the offenders will be killed for their crimes. After that proclamation, Benvolio visits his melancholy cousin Romeo whose heart is heavy with sadness. Romeo explains that he loves a woman named Rosaline but she has given her life to the Church. Benvolio attempts to make Romeo feel better, but to no avail. The cousins are approached by a Capulet servant who cannot read and they are accidentally invited to a party at the Capulet mansion. Though Romeo is reluctant to go to a party where he could potentially forget about Rosaline, Benvolio eventually convinces him to go.

Romeo is initially miserable at the party but his demeanor changes when he catches Juliet's gaze. At first, Juliet attempts to subvert Romeo's lust by speaking of holy pilgrims, but it does not take long for Romeo to convince her that even saints experience love. Juliet quickly abandons her previous beliefs and follows Romeo's impetuous lead. In a matter of moments, they fall deeply in love. However, neither of them realizes that they are in love with their mortal enemy. After they are torn apart by Romeo's rapid exit, both lovers realize their plights. Even their knowledge cannot stop their love and Romeo risks his life to visit Juliet that night. In the infamous balcony scene, Romeo and Juliet exchange vows of love. Juliet promises to send her Nurse to find Romeo the next day so they can discuss the subject of marriage. With a kiss and eager anticipation, Romeo and Juliet say farewell for the night.

Despite the fact that Romeo and Juliet think they have their futures planned, the forces that will ultimately drag them apart are already at work. A young man named Paris asks Juliet's father Capulet for permission to marry Juliet. Capulet advises Paris to wait on the marriage because Juliet is a mere 12-years-old, but he also tells Paris that the party will be the perfect opportunity for him to woo her. Meanwhile, Juliet's cousin Tybalt spots Romeo at the party and considers his presence to be an insult to the Capulet family. At that moment, Tybalt vows revenge on Romeo. Before the young lovers even have a chance to experience a true relationship, forces of fate are already tearing them apart.

The morning after the party, Romeo visits with Friar Lawrence to make arrangements for a wedding. Friar Lawrence initially thinks that this wedding is a terrible idea because it has only been a matter of hours since Romeo was in love with Rosaline. Romeo explains that his feelings for Rosaline were not real love and that he wishes to marry "the fair daughter of rich Capulet." Under the belief that this wedding could end the feud between the two prominent families, Friar Lawrence consents to marry the young lovers. Soon after, Juliet's Nurse seeks out Romeo in secrecy. Romeo advises her to prepare Juliet for confession so that they can be married right away. Friar Lawrence performs the wedding ceremony in front of Juliet's Nurse and Romeo's servant Balthasar. Now husband and wife, Romeo and Juliet arrange to meet in Juliet's bedroom that night.

After the wedding, Romeo rushes to see his cousin Benvolio. Before he can tell them about the wedding, Tybalt arrives to get his revenge on Romeo. Since he now considers himself a part of Tybalt's family, Romeo tries to avoid the inevitable fight. Disgusted by Romeo's refusal to fight, Mercutio engages in a duel with Tybalt. Romeo tries to stop Mercutio before he kills Tybalt, but Tybalt uses that opportunity to stab Mercutio. As he is dying, Mercutio curses both households. Torn with grief, Romeo retaliates by killing Tybalt. With Tybalt's blood on his hands, Romeo shouts that he is "fortune's fool." He flees from the scene and hides at Friar Lawrence's cell.

Upon arriving at the scene, the Prince declares that Romeo is banished. When Friar Lawrence tells Romeo of this news, Romeo is devastated. Since he will surely be killed if he stays in Verona, Romeo plans to leave for Mantua. First he visits Juliet in her chambers and spends his only night with his wife. In the morning, Romeo leaves Juliet against his will and travels to Mantua.

Soon after Romeo leaves, Juliet's mother attempts to cheer Juliet up by telling her that she will become Paris' wife in a few days. When Juliet becomes angry and refuses her mother's orders, Juliet's parents cannot understand her insolence. Her parents tell Juliet that she has no choice but to marry Paris. To Juliet's horror, the Nurse agrees. Overcome with fear, Juliet visits Friar Lawrence and threatens to commit suicide if she must marry Paris. Friar Lawrence formulates a plan and gives Juliet a potion that will make her look like she is dead. He advises her to drink the potion the night before her upcoming wedding. While her family sends her to the Capulet tomb, Friar Lawrence will send for Romeo so the two can be reunited and flee together. Juliet takes the vial out of desperation and says her unbeknownst goodbyes to her family.

The night before her wedding, Juliet drinks the potion. As Friar Lawrence predicted, everybody thinks that she is dead. Unfortunately, one of these people is Balthasar and he rushes to tell Romeo the bad news. Friar Lawrence's letter never gets to Romeo and Romeo believes that Juliet truly died. Romeo flees to the apothecary and purchases a vial of deadly poison. After saying his final goodbye to Juliet, Romeo drinks the poison. Mere moments later, Juliet awakens and finds her dead husband's body lying next to her. She ignores Friar Lawrence's pleas for her to leave and she plunges a dagger into her heart. Now that both lovers are dead, Friar Lawrence tells the families the entire story. The mutual grief that the families share puts an end to their feud. Thus Romeo and Juliet eventually brought peace, but it was at the price of their lives.

The Faerie Queen

"The Faerie Queen" was written by Edmund Spenser in the late 17th century. Although it was never actually completed, it is still one of the longest works of English poetry. The poem is divided up into several "books."

Each book focuses on a different virtue by telling the story of a different knight and a quest that they must complete. For example, the first book is the story of Redcrosse and considers the virtue of Holiness. Other books have themes of temperance, chastity, friendship, justice and courtesy.

The Faerie Queen also stands as a strong religious and political commentary. One of Spenser's motives in writing the poem was as a compliment the monarch Queen Elizabeth, and it boldly claims a connection between her linage and that of King Arthur. Queen Elizabeth is equated with the Faerie Queen Gloriana. The poem also holds repeated criticisms of Catholicism and instead favors the prevailing Protestantism of the time.

Age of Enlightenment

The Age of Enlightenment marks a period between the end of the 17th and 18th centuries that was set apart by dramatic social and political upheaval. Both the American and the French Revolutions took place during this period. It also saw the beginning of the Industrial Revolution in England. These events also caused changes in the literature of the time.

Ideas of what it meant to be a person and what rights and responsibilities people had to one another and to their country became a major focus of literature and philosophy during the Age of Enlightenment. Writers such as Voltaire and Jean-Jacques Rousseau questioned the status quo and some political-minded authors, such as Daniel Dafoe, began exploring ideas through novels.

Satire was also popular in literature at the time. One of the best examples of satire during the period was Jonathan Swift's *A Modest Proposal* which was published in 1729.

The Age of Enlightenment also saw the beginnings of three new literary forms: Gothic novels, melodrama, and science fiction. The first Gothic novel in English was Horace Walpole's *The Castle of Otranto* in 1764. Melodramas (known then as domestic tragedies), now common on television, began during this period with *The London Merchant*, a play by George Lillo in 1731. Finally, while science fiction wasn't fully developed as a genre during the Age of Enlightenment, Voltaire's work *Micromegas* about space travelers who land on Earth was one of the earliest examples of the form.

Among the most well-known writings of the Age of Enlightenment are the following:

- *Robinson Crusoe* and *Moll Flanders* by Daniel Dafoe

- *Gulliver's Travels* and *A Modest Proposal* by Jonathan Swift

- *A Treatise of Human Nature* by David Hume

- *Tom Jones* by Henry Fielding

- *Candide* by Voltaire

- *Emile* by Jean-Jacques Rousseau

- *The Castle of Otranto* by Horace Walpole

- *Poems* by Thomas Gray

- *An Essay on Criticism* by Alexander Pope

- *Common Sense* by Thomas Paine

Romantic Period

As the Age of Enlightenment was drawing to a close, the Romantic Period began. While the works of Rousseau may have inspired some of the ideas for the Romantic Period, the first recognized work of the period was Johann Wolfgang von Goethe's *The Sorrows of Young Werther* in 1774.

Much of the material created during the Romantic Period was a reaction to the upheaval of the Age of Enlightenment. There was an emphasis on freedom, imagination, and emotion. Nature plays an enormous role in Romantic Period literature as well.

The Romantic Period, which is considered to have begun in the late 18th century and to have continued through the first part of the 19th century, saw a resurgence in the popularity of poetry and the division of literature into separate genres, such as Gothic, science fiction, etc.

The movement was largely a reaction against the Enlightenment ideals, and shifted focus from science and reason, to individuality, nature, and emotion. Ideals such as imagination and simplicity began to take a stronger root, and beauty was seen as important. Poetry was the most popular writing style, although aspects of Romantic thought penetrated to all forms of writing and art during the period. Thomas Carlyle, John Stuart Mills, and John Ruskin were three popular authors of the Romantic era.

Poets, such as William Wordsworth and William Blake, were spreading Romantic ideals through their collections. Lord Byron, Percy Bysshe Shelly, and John Keats were creating other notable examples of Romantic poetry during this time.

Novelists were also becoming more common and more popular. In France, Victor Hugo was a notable success. In Britain, Mary Shelley published *Frankenstein*, which is now considered the first true science fiction novel. Another female author, Jane Austen, was also publishing her novels, including *Emma* and *Mansfield Park*.

One of the other developments during the Romantic Period was the growth of literature in the United States. Many of the short stories, poems, and novels produced in the United States during this time would fit into the Gothic genre, including the works of Edgar Allan Poe, Nathaniel Hawthorne, and Washington Irving. One exception was James Fenimore Cooper, most well-known as the author of *The Last of the Mohicans*, whose works described the American frontier and developed the idea of the "noble savage."

Two of the most well-known authors of the Romantic period were Charles Lamb and William Wordsworth. Although Lamb is primarily known for his prose writing, and Wordsworth for his poetry, the two held an extensive correspondence and were instrumental in bringing about the Romantic movement. Despite their similar opinions and styles, the two were not without disagreements.

In a famous letter from Charles Lamb to William Wordsworth, Lamb offers a satiric criticism of country lifestyle. Instead, Lamb extols the virtues of the ever changing, exciting city of London (in which he was born and died). Lamb even praises the less reputable aspects of the city as an essential element of the life of the city. Although he sends his "kindest love," Lamb declines an invitation to leave the city for Wordsworth's country life.

The works of Americans such as Emily Dickinson, Walt Whitman, and Herman Melville also captured the essence of the Romantic Period. During this period in America, Ralph Waldo Emerson and Henry David Thoreau were also developing the concept of Transcendentalism in their writings.

Among the most well-known writings of the Romantic Period are the following:

- *Lyrical Ballads* by William Wordsworth and Samuel Taylor Coleridge

- *Songs of Innocence* by William Blake

- *Don Juan* by Lord Byron

- "Prometheus Unbound" by Percy Bysshe Shelley

- "Ode to a Grecian Urn" by John Keats

- *Frankenstein* by Mary Shelley

- *The Hunchback of Notre Dame* and *Les Miserables* by Victor Hugo

- *Legend of Sleepy Hollow* by Washington Irving

- *The House of the Seven Gables* by Nathaniel Hawthorne

- *The Last of the Mohicans* by James Fenimore Cooper

- "The Raven" and "The Fall of the House of Usher" by Edgar Allan Poe

- *Moby Dick* by Herman Melville

- *Walden* and "Civil Disobedience" by Henry David Thoreau

- "Concord Hymn" and Nature by Ralph Waldo Emerson

- *Leaves of Grass* by Walt Whitman

- "The Song of Hiawatha" by Henry Wadsworth Longfellow

- *A Critique of Pure Reason* by Immanuel Kant

- *The Sorrows of Young Werther* by Johann Wolfgang von Goethe

- *A Vindication of the Rights of Women* by Mary Wollstonecraft

- *Sense and Sensibility* by Jane Austen

- *The Vampyre* by John William Polidori

- *Rob Roy* and *Ivanhoe* by Sir Walter Scott

- *Count of Monte Cristo* by Alexandre Dumas

Pre-Raphaelites

The Pre-Raphaelites, or Pre-Raphaelite Brotherhood, was established in 1849. The purpose of the brotherhood was originally a deliberate movement to change artistic views of the day. For several centuries the primary inspirations had been classical, such as that of Raphael. The Pre-Raphaelites advocated a brighter and more detail-oriented style of artwork.

Whereas the style of the day favored muted colors, and clear light sources on one side of the painting, the Pre-Raphaelites advocated an evenly lit and brightly colored style. These styles also carried over into the poetry of the day. Followers of pre-Raphaelite philosophy were very descriptive, sensual, and detail oriented in their writing as well.

A periodical known as *The Germ* was even founded during this time, although it published only four editions. The brotherhood was initially founded by William Holman Hunt, John Everett Millais, and Dante Gabriel Rossetti. The three were later joined by four others, bringing the total of the brotherhood to seven. However, by the end of the century the movement had faded away.

Picaresque

A picaresque novel was an early form of novel that takes its name from Spanish origins. It derives from a word meaning rogue or rascal. The central plot of a picaresque is a depiction of a low-born, roguish character as they go about their life and attempt to survive. Picaresques address the issues and corruption of life as the main figure goes from trouble to trouble barely escaping due to his own lies, thievery, deceptions and other immoral acts. The picaresque style contrasts sharply with the epic poetry and noble heroes of the medieval period. The style was popular beginning in Spain in the 16th century, and it spread through Europe through the 18th century.

 Realism

From the middle of the 19th century to the beginning of the 20th, Queen Victoria ruled Britain; therefore, this time period is sometimes known as the Victorian Era.

The literature of the time seems to be a dichotomy between realism, a movement developed in Europe and in the United States, and a continuation of elements from the Romantic Period. This same opposition was apparent in Victorian society where morals and proper behavior were stressed while the Industrial Revolution brought increased poverty and hardship, including child labor, to the cities.

Writers tried to illustrate these social problems in a realistic way, as Charles Dickens did in his novels *David Copperfield*, *Oliver Twist*, and *Great Expectations*. George Eliot, whose real name was Mary Ann Evans, took a realistic approach to British society, politics, and psychological insight in her novel *Middlemarch*.

Eliot's work may have been more in touch with the realism movement, but other writers during the time continued some of the traditions of the Romantic Period, particularly its Gothic elements. Charlotte Bronte's *Jane Eyre* and Emily Bronte's *Wuthering Heights* are two examples.

In the United States, the Civil War and its aftermath paved the way for more realism authors, including *Mark Twain* and *Henry James*.

Some writers of the time were also creating controversy by questioning some of the social norms of their time. Oscar Wilde's *The Importance of Being Earnest* was a satire of the upper classes during the Victorian Era. Henrik Ibsen's *A Doll's House* questioned the roles of men and women in society and in marriage. Thomas Hardy's *Tess of the d'Urbervilles* and *Jude the Obscure* also created controversy with their depictions of women and of marriage.

Not all writers during the period were interested in realism or controversy. Sir Arthur Conan Doyle wrote and published four novels and more than four dozen short stories about Sherlock Holmes during this time. Lewis Carroll, whose real name was Charles Lutwidge Dodgson, published both *Alice's Adventures in Wonderland* and *Through the Looking Glass*. Robert Louis Stevenson wrote several adventure books, including *Treasure Island*, as well as the horror novel *The Body Snatcher*. Stevenson's other famous work, *The Strange Case of Dr. Jekyll and Mr. Hyde*, explored the inner workings of the human mind, which was also a common theme in the works of James and Eliot.

Matthew Arnold was a famed author and poet near the end of the Victorian Era, and is considered the third great poet of the era (along with Lord Alfred Tennyson and Robert Browning). One of his most famous passages is from a long poem entitled Stanzas from the Great Chartreuse. The Great Chartreuse was a castle that Arnold visited, and the poem was written while he was there. The most famous passage reads "Between two worlds, one dead/ The other powerless to be born/ With nowhere yet to rest my head/ Like these, on earth I wait forlorn." Much of his work displayed an anxiety about the changing ideals of his time. Although he witnessed a beginning of abandonment of Victorian ideals, he was not comfortable with what they should or could be replaced with. Much of his writing took on a solemn tone. He was very concerned with social matters, and advocated social criticism.

Poetry was still an important part of the literature during the age of Realism. Robert Browning found success with his lengthy poem "The Ring and the Book." Alfred Tennyson revisited the Greek classics with his poems "Ulysses" and "The Lotus Eaters."

Among the most well-known writings of Realism are the following:

- *Middlemarch* by George Eliot

- *Great Expectations*, *David Copperfield*, *Oliver Twist*, and *A Tale of Two Cities* by Charles Dickens

- *The Adventures of Sherlock Holmes* and *The Hound of the Baskervilles* by Sir Arthur Conan Doyle

- *The Importance of Being Earnest* and *The Picture of Dorian Gray* by Oscar Wilde

- *Jane Eyre* by Charlotte Bronte

- *Wuthering Heights* by Emily Bronte

- *Alice's Adventures in Wonderland* and *Through the Looking Glass* by Lewis Carroll

- *Treasure Island* and *The Strange Case of Dr. Jekyll and Mr. Hyde* by Robert Louis Stevenson

- *Tess of the d'Urbervilles* and *Jude the Obscure* by Thomas Hardy

- *A Doll's House* by Henrik Ibsen

- *The Ring and the Book* by Robert Browning

- *The Turn of the Screw* and *Portrait of a Lady* by Henry James

- *Adventures of Huckleberry Finn* and *The Adventures of Tom Sawyer* by Mark Twain.

- *Anna Karenina* and *War and Peace* by Leo Tolstoy

- *Madame Bovary* by Gustave Flaubert

- *Lady Chatterley's Lover* and *Sons and Lovers* by D. H. Lawrence

Naturalism

After Charles Darwin's 1859 publication of *The Origin of Species*, many writers and thinkers were inspired to take a new approach to their work. This approach, which began in France in the late 19th century, known as Naturalism, spread throughout the rest of the Western world.

Unlike realism, which wanted to capture true life experiences and sights on paper, naturalism instead sought to take an objective view of human beings and their relationships. Naturalism also focused on the forces surrounding and influencing human life and behavior, such as the age-old question of nature versus nurture. Naturalist writers also presented the natural world as cold and indifferent to humans, which was a sharp contrast from the way nature was portrayed by romantic period writers.

In France, one of the most celebrated naturalist writers was Emile Zola. He released 20 novels known collectively as Les Rougon-Macquart. While his work went on to influence many French writers, including Guy de Maupassant, other naturalist writers were producing works in the United States.

Some of the most well-known American authors of the late 19th and early 20th centuries were naturalist writers, including John Steinbeck, Jack London, Stephen Crane, Theodore Dreiser, Richard Wright, and Edith Wharton.

Among the most well-known writings of Naturalism are the following:

- *Sister Carrie* by Theodore Dreiser

- *The Grapes of Wrath* and *The Pearl* by John Steinbeck

- *The Call of the Wild* and *White Fang* by Jack London

- *The Red Badge of Courage* and *Maggie: A Girl of the Streets* by Stephen Crane

- *Native Son* and *Black Boy* by Richard Wright

- *The House of Mirth* by Edith Wharton

- *Les Rougon-Macquart* by Emile Zola

Modernism

Near the end of Naturalism's reign in literature, a new movement began to spring up. This movement, known as Modernism, lasted from around 1910 through the post World War II years. One of the Modernist's complaints about Realist writing was that it lacked the emotion necessary to fully capture a traumatic experience, such as being on the front line during World War I. Modernism was also heavily influenced by a number of key events, including both World Wars, the rise of Fascism in parts of Europe, the growing interest in Marxism (inspired by Karl Marx and Friedrich Engel's The Communist Manifesto published in 1848), and the Great Depression.

Modernism in literature rebuked the need for rigid forms or conventions. Instead, the emphasis was on freedom of expression and experimentation. This emphasis can best be illustrated by the stream of consciousness writings of James Joyce and Virginia Woolf. Other writers, such as Franz Kafka and William Faulkner, also tried new approaches in their works.

One of the key elements of Modernist thought was a sense of alienation from one's true self or from the society in which one lived. This element was developed further in the dystopian novels of George Orwell and Aldous Huxley.

Because of the Modernist emphasis on politics, radicalism, and free expression, it was rejected by many of the powerful governments of the time, including Nazi Germany and the Soviet Union.

Among the most well-known writings of Modernism are the following:

- *The Waste Land* by T. S. Eliot

- *1984* and *Animal Farm* by George Orwell

- *The Cantos* by Ezra Pound

- *The Heart of Darkness* by Joseph Conrad

- *Mrs. Dalloway* by Virginia Woolf

- *A Room of One's Own* by Virginia Woolf

- "The Metamorphosis" by Franz Kafka

- *Brave New World* by Aldous Huxley

- *A Farewell To Arms* and *For Whom the Bell Tolls* by Ernest Hemingway

- *Ulysses* and *Finnegan's Wake* by James Joyce

- *The Sound and the Fury* and *As I Lay Dying* by William Faulkner

Postmodernism

While many literary movements replaced or rebuked the ones that came before it, post-modernism is actually an outgrowth of modernism. In fact, many of the same elements and themes can be seen in works by authors falling into both camps.

Postmodernism began after World War II and many of the writers from this movement continue writing and publishing currently as well, even though the movement does not have the same popularity it once did.

Like modernism, postmodernism seems to emphasize irony and parody as a way to address issues related to the self and to society. The main difference between the two movements is the way they view the sense of alienation felt by people in the 20th century. Modernists see their art as a way to bring unity to themselves so that they are either closer to themselves or to their society. Postmodernists celebrate their feelings of alienation and infuse with their works with those types of ideas.

Postmodernism, perhaps even more than modernism, is also experimental and does not follow the typical conventions. Many writers also have chosen to deal with controversial themes and plots, such as Vladimir Nabokov's *Lolita*.

Among the most well-known writings of Postmodernism are the following:

- *On the Road* by Jack Kerouac

- *Howl* by Allen Ginsberg

- *The Naked Lunch* by William Burroughs

- *Lolita* by Vladimir Nabokov

- *The Crying of Lot 49* and *Gravity's Rainbow* by Thomas Pynchon

- *Players* and *White Noise* by Don Delillo

- *Less Than Zero* and *American Psycho* by Bret Easton Ellis

- *Time's Arrow* and *London Fields* by Martin Amis

- *The End of the Road* and *Lost in the Funhouse* by John Barth

- *Still Life With Woodpecker* by Tom Robbins

Richard Cory

Edwin Arlington Robinson was considered to be one of the greatest American poets of his time. Robinson was born in Maine in 1869 and died in the midst of the Great Depression in 1935. Due to the hardships of the depression, much of his work focused on themes of poverty. Robinson particularly wrote about situations in which all was not as it seemed and where money didn't bring happiness. One of his most famous works is the poem "Richard Cory." The poem describes how the destitute townspeople would look up to the wealthy Richard Cory each day, and envy his riches. They idolized him as being greater than a king. Then one summer night Richard Cory kills himself. Through the poem, Robinson shows that wealth does not bring happiness, and that human companionship is far more important to a successful life. Although Richard Cory may have appeared to have everything in life – he was clean, healthy, and a gentleman – in truth he was not happy at all.

Essayists

Charles Lamb was an English essayist in the early 1800s.

Thomas De Quincey was a English essayist. His most famous work is *Confessions of an English Opium-Eater* (1821).

Women Writers

There have been many influential and popular women writers throughout the centuries.

Margaret Atwood is a renowned Canadian author and poet. Atwood was born in Toronto in 1939 and knew at a very young age that she wished to be a professional writer. After studying for several years at Victoria College in the University of Toronto Atwood began graduate studies at Radcliffe College, earning a master's degree by 1962. She is well-known for her feminist attitudes in her writing, and has successfully published in a variety of genres.

She has received several science fiction awards for her novels, although she claims that they are not science fiction. Atwood prefers the designation of speculative fiction, claiming that there is a difference between writing about things that can't happen, science fiction, and things that haven't happened, speculative fiction. Atwood is also known for inventing the LongPen – a mechanical signing device that allowed her to sign using a mechanical arm without being physically present.

Christina Rossetti was a famous author of the Pre-Raphaelite movement which was largely founded by her brother Dante Rossetti. A common theme of Christina Rossetti's work was feminism. In particular, she often speculated about her place as a female poet, and the place of women in society in general. One of her famous works touching on this subject is the poem "In An Artist's Studio." The poem describes an artist's studio which is filled with work, but notes that each piece reflects the same female subject. The poem implies that this has the effect of imprisoning the woman. Rather than freeing her, she becomes a slave to the perceptions of the artist. Like many of her other works, the poem was not published until after Rossetti's death in 1894.

However, she continues to be considered one of the great female authors along with Emily Dickinson and Elizabeth Browning. She is also famous for her poetry which includes the words to the Christmas carol "In the Bleak Midwinter."

Katherine Mansfield wrote short fiction in the early 1900s. A native of New Zeland, she contracted TB which led to her early death at 34.

Literary Criticism

The practice of literary criticism has been around since the creation of the first book. Literary criticism revolves around the idea of interpreting, analyzing, and critiquing an author's work, usually according to a specific literary theory. Literary theory is the idea of what literature should accomplish and how those goals should be accomplished by the author.

Below we will discuss some of the more common literary theories that have and continue to be used during literary criticism discussions.

Psychoanalytic Theory

In the late 19th century, the work of Sigmund Freud was revolutionizing the way people thought of themselves and their minds. Freud, and his protege Carl Jung, both carried over the ideas of psychoanalysis into the study of literature as well.

Essentially, the same tools and concepts that are used by psychoanalysts to evaluate a patient can also be used to further understand a work's author, primary characters, or even its audience.

This idea of evaluating a work in these terms is still common and is often connected with other literary theories. However, the modern approach is often more concerned with the psychology of the reader, not the author or the characters.

Influential Psychoanalytic Critics:

- Sigmund Freud

- Carl Jung

- Northrop Frye

- Jacques Lacan

Formalist Theory

While literary theories may seem to be harmless methods of digging deeper into literature, some theories were viewed as dangerous to society. Formalism would fall into that category.

Formalism was first introduced in Russia in 1915. Its main focus was on the purpose of literature: to help readers defamiliarize themselves with the world around them so that they could see it clearly. The idea was that once you were in a society or situation for too long you would stop seeing it as it really was, and stop questioning what was considered acceptable by the society. Literature and art, according to formalists, was created to combat that tendency.

As a result, Joseph Stalin began cracking down on formalist writers in 1930, which prevented many of their works from being published and caused others to focus less on literary criticism and more on other types of writing. Over 30 years later, translations of their works began to appear in the West.

Influential Formalist Critics:

• Victor Shklovsky

• Yuri Tynyanov

• Vladimir Propp

New Criticism Theory

New Criticism began around the same time as Formalism, but it took a different approach. While both schools of criticism believed that close reading of the text was important, New Critics saw the literature itself as a way to further one's understanding of the world.

New Critics were also very strict about how meaning could be perceived in a text. The author's intended meaning wasn't important, because it could never truly be known. All that mattered were the meanings found in the text itself. New Critics also believed that every text contained multiple meanings that co-existed simultaneously.

New Criticism continued to be popular up through the 1960's.

Influential New Critics:

• T. S. Eliot

• W. K. Wimsatt

• I. A. Richards

Reader Response Theory

In the 1940's a new area of literary theory began to become popular. This theory became known as Reader Response.

Reader Response theorists believe the only meaning in a piece of literature is the meaning created by the reader's interaction with the text. The author's intended meaning and even the meaning of the words themselves are not important.

The crux of the Reader Response argument is that each reader brings his or her own frame of reference to a text. Readers' culture, history, language, and psychology all impact what they get out of the text. According to the theory, two separate individuals could read the same text and derive two completely different meanings from them.

Currently, Reader Response theory is closely linked to Psychoanalytic Theory.

Influential Reader Response Critics:

• Stanley Fish

• Wolfgang Iser

 # *Structuralist Theory*

After World War II, another approach to literary theory began to pick up speed in popularity. Known as structuralism, the ideas of these theorists were first used in the study of linguistics to break down the language into its smallest possible parts.

They then used similar rules to examine literature. Each action or narrative in a work by itself, according to theorists, needs to be analyzed, but that's only part of the puzzle. The next part is looking carefully at how all of those small pieces come together in the work.

While Structuralism was quite popular up through the early 60's, it lost popularity as the 1970's began.

Influential Structuralist Critics:

• Roland Barthes

- Umberto Eco

- Claude Levi-Strauss

Feminist Theory

Although a Feminist approach to literature had been around since the early 20th century, it wasn't until the Feminist Movement began that this school of literary criticism became popular.

Unlike other theories, Feminist Theory can't be condensed into a single idea. Instead, it includes several ideas and approaches to literature. Some theorists focus on sexual differences described in literature while others focus on the sexual stereotypes found in works.

Other Feminist Theorists try to rediscover female literature from the past or to re-interpret older works in terms of more modern ideas. Feminist Theorists are also typically outspoken about the historic oppression of women in literature.

Influential Feminist Critics:

- Elaine Showalter

- Annette Kolodny

- Virginia Woolf

- Simone de Beauvoir

Marxist Theory

In the 1970's, literary theory turned towards the teachings of Karl Marx for guidance and a new approach to finding meaning in literature was born.

While Marxism itself is about developing a social system based on equality, Marxist Theorists believe that all literary meaning is determined by historic and economic conditions. Therefore, to understand literature, we must understand the time period in which it was written.

Marxist Theory in terms of literary criticism is still used, especially in connection with Deconstruction and Feminist Theory.

Influential Marxist Critics:

* Raymond Williams

* Edmund Wilson

Deconstructive Theory

From the late 1960's to the present, deconstruction has been the predominant theory in literary criticism. It was initially started by Jacques Derrida, who remains one of the most influential deconstructive thinkers.

Deconstructionists focus on closely reading texts and looking for opposition between the words in the piece and the piece's meaning. According to these theorists, the true meaning of the works comes from examining these contradictions.

Modern deconstruction theory is often teamed up with other theories, such as Feminism and Marxism.

Influential Deconstructive Critics:

* Geoffrey Hartman

* Barbara Johnson

# Everyman

The Middle English play known as *Everyman* is a common example of a morality play. The play addresses the common medieval theme of death. In the beginning God speaks and mourns that mankind has forgotten to be God-fearing. He announces that Death is the great messenger that determines whether a person has done good or evil. Everyman is told by Death that he must take his journey with a "book of count." As Everyman proceeds on his journey to death, he seeks to bring others along with him – discretion, knowledge, confession, strength, beauty, and kindred – but all abandon him in the end. As he goes to his grave, only Good Deeds remains with Everyman. The message of the play is a warning that all but good deeds will abandon every man in the end.

Non-fiction

The first American dictionary was written by Samuel Johnson. Prior to Johnson there was no consistency to the written English language. However, with growing literacy and ease of publishing, Johnson was commissioned to make the language more accessible to the average person. A similar work had been undertaken by the French Academy and taken over forty years to complete. Johnson was able to accomplish the task in ten. His dictionary, called A Dictionary of the English Language or Johnson's Dictionary, held of 40,000 entries with extensive references and definitions. The dictionary was published in 1775.

James Boswell wrote a biography on Samuel Johnson.

Two famous and influential diarists were **Samuel Pepys** and **John Evelyn**. Their diaries or memoirs have been preserved, along with much of their correspondence.

Reading List

In addition to all the links in the guide, make sure you at least read the SUMMARIES. You NEED to know the summaries and characters to be able to pass the test:

The Way of All Flesh http://www.bibliomania.com/0/0/10/18/frameset.html

Alice Through the Looking Glass http://www.cs.indiana.edu/metastuff/looking/lookingdir.html

Gulliver's Travels http://en.wikipedia.org/wiki/Gulliver%27s_travels

The Pilgrims Progress http://www.ccel.org/ccel/bunyan/pilgrim.iii.html

Robinson Crusoe http://en.wikipedia.org/wiki/Robinson_Crusoe

Julius Caesar http://en.wikipedia.org/wiki/Julius_Caesar_(play)

King Lear http://en.wikipedia.org/wiki/King_lear

Henry IV http://www.shakespeare-online.com/quotes/1henryivquotes.html

Paradise Lost http://en.wikipedia.org/wiki/Paradise_lost

The Love Song of J. Alfred Prufrock http://www.bartleby.com/198/1.html

Ulysses http://en.wikipedia.org/wiki/Ulysses

A Valediction Forbidding Morning http://www.luminarium.org/sevenlit/donne/mourning.htm

The Rubáiyát of Omar Kayyám http://www.okonlife.com/poems/

A Portrait of the Artist as a Young Man http://en.wikipedia.org/wiki/A_Portrait_of_the_Artist_as_a_Young_Man

The Waste Land http://en.wikipedia.org/wiki/The_waste_land

The Rime of the Ancient Mariner http://en.wikipedia.org/wiki/The_Rime_of_the_Ancient_Mariner

Songs of Innocence http://en.wikipedia.org/wiki/Songs_of_Innocence

The Faerie Queene http://en.wikipedia.org/wiki/The_Faerie_Queene

The Rape of the Lock http://en.wikipedia.org/wiki/The_Rape_of_the_Lock

Tess of the D'Uberville http://www.allreaders.com/Topics/info_8267.asp?BSID=22772876

Sons and Lovers http://en.wikipedia.org/wiki/Sons_and_lovers

Professions for Women http://ebooks.adelaide.edu.au/w/woolf/virginia/w91d/chapter27.html

Lycidas http://www.bartleby.com/101/317.html

The Canonization http://www.luminarium.org/sevenlit/donne/canonization.htm

Pride and Prejudice http://en.wikipedia.org/wiki/Pride_and_Prejudice

The Rover http://www.enotes.com/rover/

The Rivals http://www.curtainup.com/b-rivals.html

She Stoops to Conquer http://www.bartleby.com/18/3/

As You Like It http://en.wikipedia.org/wiki/As_You_Like_It

Lord Jim http://www.online-literature.com/conrad/lord_jim/

Briefing for a Descent into Hell http://www.dorislessing.org/briefingfor.html

A Passage to India http://en.wikipedia.org/wiki/A_Passage_to_India

Riders to the Sea http://www.theatrehistory.com/irish/synge002.html

Equus http://en.wikipedia.org/wiki/Equus_(play)

Waiting for Godot http://en.wikipedia.org/wiki/Waiting_for_Godot

Look Back in Anger http://www.enotes.com/look-back-anger/

Murder in the Cathedral http://www.enotes.com/murder-cathedral/

The Golden Notebook http://www.bookrags.com/shortguide-golden_notebook/

Elegy Written in a Country Churchyard http://www.bartleby.com/101/453.html

Sample Test Questions

For the short stories in this section, please refer to the appendix located at the back of the study guide.

I. LITERATURE

A. Read Ernest Hemingway's short story "The Short Happy Life of Francis Macomber" then choose the best answer to the following questions:

1) Which of the following is the theme of this story?

   A) Hunting
   B) Deterioration of a marriage
   C) Adultery
   D) Murder
   E) Marriage

The correct answer is B:) Deterioration of a marriage.

2) Which best describes the setting?

   A) African safari
   B) Emotional tension (between Macomber and Margot)
   C) Ego relations between a man and woman
   D) Hunting wild game
   E) All of the above

The correct answer is C:) Ego relations between a man and woman.

3) Which best describes the style of writing?

   A) Indirect
   B) Wordy, long-winded
   C) Highly economical
   D) Words flow slowly and lazily
   E) Victorian

The correct answer is C:) Highly economical.

4) What device does the author use primarily to reveal character?

    A) Long, detailed descriptions
    B) Their actions
    C) Their inner thoughts
    D) The clothes they wore
    E) Their dialogue

The correct answer is B:) Their actions.

5) At what point does the climax occur in this story?

    A) When Macomber flees from the wounded lion
    B) When Margot shoots him
    C) When Margot goes to visit Wilson in his tent
    D) When Macomber "comes into his own" and finds courage in the excitement of the chase
    E) When Wilson treats him like a comrade

The correct answer is D:) When Macomber "comes into his own" and finds courage in the excitement of the chase.

6) What is the denouement of the story? (The point at which all issues are resolved.)

    A) When Macomber "comes into his own" and finds courage in the excitement of the chase
    B) When Wilson accuses Margot of murder
    C) When Margot shoots Macomber
    D) When Wilson congratulates Macomber on finding his manhood
    E) When the two men hunt together

The correct answer is C:) When Margot shoots Macomber.

B. Read Edgar Allen Poe's short story "The Fall of the House of Usher," and choose the best answer to the following questions:

1) What does the house symbolize?

   A) Roderick, the current inhabitant
   B) The Usher family
   C) The illness of Roderick and his sister
   D) The narrator
   E) The area where it was located

The correct answer is B:) The Usher family.

2) Poe felt that the "tale" made possible the "fairest field for the exercise of the loftiest talent." He also wrote, "the unity of effect or impression is a point of the greatest importance." What "effect" or "impression" does this author strive for in this story?

   A) Happy
   B) Angry
   C) Impending doom
   D) Friendly
   E) Scary

The correct answer is C:) Impending doom.

3) What is the *most important* means that the author uses to achieve this effect?

   A) Descriptions
   B) The history of the family
   C) The reactions of the narrator
   D) The supernatural happenings
   E) The description of the house when the narrator arrives

The correct answer is E:) The description of the house when the narrator arrives.

4) What is the *most important* device that the author uses to reveal character?

    A) Physical description
    B) Their conversations
    C) Statement by the narrator
    D) Dialogue
    E) Supernatural happenings

The correct answer is C:) Statement by the narrator.

5) What is the point of view of this story?

    A) Third person omniscient
    B) Third person
    C) Second person
    D) First person narrator objective
    E) First person narrator omniscient

The correct answer is E:) First person narrator omniscient.

6) What are the major conflicts in this story?

    A) The narrator vs. the inhabitants of the house
    B) Roderick vs. his sister
    C) The Ushers vs. ultimate annihilation
    D) The house vs. the inhabitants
    E) The narrator vs. the house

The correct answer is C:) The Ushers vs. ultimate annihilation.

7) By what specific devices is an identification between Roderick Usher and the house achieved?

    A) The personification of the house (eye-like windows, etc.)
    B) The description of the interior of the house
    C) The dialogue between him and the narrator
    D) The relationship between Roderick and his sister.
    E) The poetry

The correct answer is A:) The personification of the house (eye-like windows, etc.).

C. Read Henry James' short story "The Real Thing" and choose the best answer to the following:

1) Irony can be described as a discrepancy between what might reasonably be expected and what actually occurs—between the appearance of a situation and its reality. Where is there irony in this story by Henry James?

 A) The clothes the Monarchs wear compared to the clothes Miss Churmwears.
 B) The "sitters" doing housework
 C) Miss Churm and Oronte posing as upper-class
 D) The inability of the Monarchs to model upper-class figures
 E) The discomfort of the narrator

The correct answer is D:) The inability of the Monarchs to model upper-class figures.

2) What is the major theme of this story?

 A) Upper class people sometimes lose their money.
 B) When upper-class people lose their money, they are helpless.
 C) Art is not a realistic picture of an object, but the creative representation of it.
 D) Lower-class people make good subjects for artists.
 E) Lower-class people do not respect upper-class people.

The correct answer is C:) Art is not a realistic picture of an object, but the creative representation of it.

3) How does irony contribute to the theme (meaning) of the story?

 A) It makes the artist look more important.
 B) It doesn't contribute—it only makes the story more interesting.
 C) It shows the difference between the upper-class and lower-class.
 D) It presents a graphic picture of the nature of art.
 E) It makes the artist look incompetent.

The correct answer is D:) It presents a graphic picture of the nature of art.

4) What are the major conflicts in this story?

    A) They are internal—the artist struggles with the true nature of art
    B) Upper-class vs. lower-class
    C) Miss Churm vs. the Monarchs
    D) Lower class people vs. the snobbery of the upper-class
    E) Between the artist and the Monarchs

The correct answer is A:) They are internal—the artist struggles with the true nature of art.

5) How does James reveal character?

    A) Physical description
    B) The perception of the narrator
    C) Dialogue
    D) The setting of the studio
    E) The paintings

The correct answer is A:) Physical description.

6) What is the climax of the action in this story?

    A) When the artist pays the Monarchs off and tells them he can't use them.
    B) When the Monarchs perceive that they have been replaced by Miss Churm and Oronte.
    C) When Mrs. Monarch arranges Miss Churm's hair.
    D) When the Monarchs take care of the kitchen for the artist.
    E) When Jack Hawley confronts the artist with the unsuitability of the drawings.

The correct answer is E:) When Jack Hawley confronts the artist with the unsuitability of the drawings.

7) What is the denouement (when all issues are resolved)?

    A) When the artist pays the Monarchs off and tells them he can't use them.
    B) When the Monarchs take care of the kitchen for the artist.
    C) When Mrs. Monarch arranges Miss Churm's hair.
    D) When Jack Hawley confronts the artist with the unsuitability of the drawings.
    E) When Orontes prepares the tea.

The correct answer is A:) When the artist pays the Monarchs off and tells them he can't use them.

D. Read Katherine Anne Porter's short story "Theft" from her anthology _Flowering Judas_ and choose the correct answer to the following questions:

1) What are the conflicts in this story?

    A) The main character vs. a thieving universe.
    B) Camilo vs. Bill.
    C) The main character vs. Camilo.
    D) The main character vs. Bill.
    E) An interior one within the character.

The correct answer is E:) An interior one within the character.

2) What is the theme?

    A) An unwillingness to protect oneself is destructive.
    B) Servants will steal if they have a chance.
    C) Friends are not to be trusted.
    D) Women need protectors.
    E) You should always lock your doors.

The correct answer is A:) An unwillingness to protect oneself is destructive.

3) What is the point of view?

> A) First person narrative.
> B) Third person narrative objective.
> C) Third person narrative omniscient.
> D) First person omniscient.
> E) Second person.

The correct answer is A:) First person narrative.

4) How does the character Camilo function in rendering the theme?

> A) He is careless about his new hat.
> B) In contrast to all the other people in her life, he is the only one who puts himself out to look after her rather than stealing from her.
> C) He is also poor.
> D) She rejects his efforts to help her.
> E) He is not attractive to her.

The correct answer is B:) In contrast to all the other people in her life, he is the only one who puts himself out to look after her rather than stealing from her.

5) What is the climax of the action?

> A) When she finds her purse missing.
> B) When she determines to get her purse back and goes to find the janitress.
> C) When the janitress brings the purse back.
> D) When she gives the purse back to the janitress.
> E) When the janitress tries to humiliate her by refusing to take the purse.

The correct answer is B:) When she determines to get her purse back and goes to find the janitress.

6) What is the denouement (when all issues are resolved)?

> A) When the janitress refuses to take the purse.
> B) When the janitress refuses to take it and insults her.
> C) When she realizes that the thief is herself.
> D) When she remembers that she has never locked doors.
> E) When she goes to the basement to the basement to confront the janitress.

The correct answer is C:) When she realizes that the thief is herself.

E. Read Hawthorne's story "Young Goodman Brown" and answer the following questions:

1) Hawthorne often used allegory in his stories, and this story is almost entirely made up of allegory. An allegory is like a parable in that it tells a story that has a second meaning. Allegories don't necessarily always have a moral although parables usually do. What is the meaning of this allegory?

    A) Those who are proponents of high standards of behavior are usually hypo-critical.
    B) Devil worship is bad.
    C) Devil worship is widespread.
    D) Husbands and wives should trust each other.
    E) Religion is not for everyone.

The correct answer is A:) Those who are proponents of high standards of behavior are usually hypocritical.

2) Hawthorne did not like the Transcendentalists of his day because he felt that their transparent optimism about the potentialities of human nature didn't match up with reality. How is that reflected in this story?

    A) Young Goodman Brown wasn't sure whether or not his visit to the forest was a dream.
    B) Faith continued to be a good wife.
    C) Young Goodman Brown snatches away a child that is being "catechized" by Goody Cloyse.
    D) He was so suspicious of everyone after his experience in the woods that his life and marriage were ruined.
    E) All the "good" people Young Goodman Brown knew had been involved in the evil meeting in the forest.

The correct answer is E:) All the "good" people Young Goodman Brown knew had been involved in the evil meeting in the forest.

3) He gave the characters names that had a function in the story. How does the name Faith function in the story?

   A) Her husband is not sure whether or not she was at the evil ceremony in the woods.
   B) The family continued to pray, but he was an unwilling participant.
   C) When he pleaded with her not to participate, his "bad dream" ended.
   D) Before Young Goodman Brown went on his journey to the woods, just as faith is to a Christian, she was the center of his existence, but after his brush with evil, even she was not a comfort to him.
   E) We are not sure whether Faith was at the devil worshipping meeting.

The correct answer is D:) Before Young Goodman Brown went on his journey to the woods, just as faith is to a Christian, she was the center of his existence, but after his brush with evil, even she was not a comfort to him.

4) This story is heavy in Biblical allusion and reference. What did the staff of the fellow traveler "which bore the likeness of a great black snake, so curiously wrought that it might almost be seen to twist and wriggle like a living serpent" signify?

   A) Evil
   B) The serpent in the Garden of Eve
   C) Aaron's rod
   D) The Devil
   E) All of the above

The correct answer is E:) All of the above.

5) Hawthorne's life was overshadowed by the fact that his grandfather had been the "hanging judge" in the Salem witch trials. He carried a heavy burden of guilt as a result of his family heritage. How is that reflected in this story?

   A) Young Goodman Brown's guilt and suspicion ruled his life after the encounter in the woods.
   B) The "evil" in this story was the practice of witchcraft.
   C) The story is set in a small New England village.
   D) There is ambivalence about the "goodness" of the church members.
   E) All of the above

The correct answer is E:) All of the above.

II. POETRY

POEM #1
Stopping by Woods on a Snowy Evening
by Robert Frost (1874-1963)

Whose woods are these I think I know.
His house is in the village though;
He will not see me stopping here
To watch his woods fill up with snow.

My little horse must think it queer
To stop without a farmhouse near
Between the woods and frozen lake
The darkest evening of the year.

He gives his harness bells a shake
To ask if there is some mistake.
The only other sound's the sweep
Of easy wind and downy flake.

The woods are lovely, dark and deep,
But I have promises to keep,
And miles to go before I sleep,
And miles to go before I sleep.

1) What is the "voice" or persona of this poem? (the speaker)

    A) A man burdened by his responsibilities
    B) A farmer
    C) A landowner
    D) A stranger
    E) A villager

The correct answer is A:) A man burdened by his responsibilities.

2) What is his attitude?

    A) He is happy.
    B) He longs to stay in the woods.
    C) He is afraid of the owner of the woods.
    D) He is impatient with his horse.
    E) He is ambivalent.

The correct answer is B:) He longs to stay in the woods.

3) What emotions is he expressing?

    A) Anger
    B) Longing
    C) Frustration
    D) Indifference
    E) Guilt

The correct answer is B:) Longing.

4) What is the theme?

    A) A ride on a snowy evening is refreshing.
    B) Taking advantage of the absence of the owner of the woods is gratifying.
    C) Responsibilities take precedence over pleasure.
    D) The beauty of nature.
    E) Animals are often impatient.

The correct answer is C:) Responsibilities take precedence over pleasure.

5) Many people who may not be able to recall the entire poem remember the last two lines. Why does he repeat the last line?

    A) He needed another line.
    B) It sounds good.
    C) It reinforces the theme.
    D) It leaves the image of life's responsibilities in the mind of the reader.
    E) It reminds the reader of the impatience of the horse.

The correct answer is C:) It reinforces the theme.

6) What does the impatient horse symbolize?

    A) The urgencies of responsibility.
    B) The poet's wife.
    C) The owner of the woods.
    D) Nature.
    E) Animals respond to people's feelings.

The correct answer is A:) The urgencies of responsibility.

7) This poem is written in perfect iambic tetrameter. How many feet are in each line?

    A) 5
    B) 4
    C) 6
    D) 3
    E) 2

The correct answer is A:) 5.

8) Robert Frost's family had many problems such as depression and suicide, and he was responsible for looking after them. He was very successful as a famous poet, teacher and editor. What is there in this poem that reflects his life?

    A) His enjoyment of nature.
    B) The statement about the owner of the farm's not knowing he was there.
    C) The desire to escape his responsibilities.
    D) The snow in the woods.
    E) He gets tired.

The correct answer is C:) The desire to escape his responsibilities.

Poem #2
A Narrow Fellow in the Grass
by Emily Dickenson (1830-1886)

A narrow fellow in the grass
Occasionally rides;
You may have met him—did you not?
His notice sudden is.

The grass divides as with a comb,
A spotted shaft is seen;
And then it closes at your feet
And opens further on.

He likes a boggy acre,
A floor too cool for corn.
Yet when a boy, and barefoot,
I more than once, at morn.

Have passed, I thought, a whip lash
Unbraiding in the sun,--
When, stooping to secure it,
It wrinkled, and was gone.

Several of nature's people
I know, and they know me;
I feel for them a transport
Of cordiality;

But never met this fellow,
Attended or alone,
Without a tighter breathing,
and Zero at the Bone.

1) The persona of a poem is often not the poet, himself or herself. Who is the persona of this poem?

    A) An old woman
    B) A barefoot boy
    C) A man
    D) A young girl
    E) A mother

The correct answer is C:) A man.

2) Who is this "narrow fellow in the grass"?

    A) A mouse
    B) A rabbit
    C) A groundhog
    D) A snake
    E) A porcupine

The correct answer is D:) A snake.

3) How does this poet feel about the "narrow fellow"?

    A) She likes him.
    B) She has no feeling about him.
    C) She is afraid of him.
    D) She avoids him.
    E) She is concerned for his welfare.

The correct answer is C:) She is afraid of him.

4) What is the theme of the poem?

    A) Some natural phenomena are intriguing but frightening.
    B) "Nature's people" should be protected.
    C) It's better to stay indoors.
    D) Animals like cool weather.
    E) Nature is beautiful.

The correct answer is A:) Some natural phenomena are intriguing but frightening.

5) A metaphor is an implied comparison. There are many metaphors in this poem. Pick the metaphor from the following list.

    A) Rides
    B) Narrow fellow
    C) Boggy acre
    D) Corn
    E) Grass divides

The correct answer is A:) Rides.

6) Pick the metaphor from this list.

    A) Whip lash
    B) Floor
    C) Tighter breathing
    D) Stooping
    E) Cordiality

The correct answer is A:) Whip lash.

7) Pick the metaphor from this list.

    A) Grass
    B) Zero at the Bone
    C) Notice
    D) Barefoot
    E) Morn

The correct answer is B:) Zero at the Bone.

8) What image does "occasionally rides" suggest?

    A) Moves along quickly
    B) Is transported on a carriage or a train
    C) Climbs into the carriage from time to time
    D) Is sometimes picked up and carried
    E) Glides

The correct answer is B:) Is transported on a carriage or a train.

9) The meter in this poem is not as regular as Frost's "Stopping by Woods. . ." What does the irregularity of rhythm do for the poem?

    A) Slows it down
    B) Makes it harder to read
    C) Reinforces the theme
    D) Doesn't make any difference
    E) Makes it rhythmic

The correct answer is C:) Reinforces the theme.

10) In the first stanza, the following pattern is found:

```
_ / _ / _ /_ /
  _ / _ / _ /
_ / _ / _ -- / _/
  _ / _ / _ /
```

What is achieved by the break in the rhythm?

    A) It slows the reader down
    B) It makes the verse seem conversational
    C) It speeds the reader up
    D) It doesn't make any difference
    E) It makes it harder to read

The correct answer is B:) It makes the verse seem conversational.

Poem #3
Pied Beauty
Gerard Manley Hopkins (1844-1889)

Glory be to God for dappled things—
    For skies of couple-colour as a brinded cow:
        For rose-moles all in stipple upon trout that swim;
Fresh-firecoal chestnut-falls; finches' wings;
    Landscape plotted and pieced—fold, fallow, and plough;
        And all the trades, their gear and tackle and trim.

All things counter, original, spare, strange;
    Whatever is fickle, freckled (who knows how?)
        With swift, slow; sweet, sour; adazzle, dim;
He fathers-forth whose beauty is past change;
            Praise him.

Gerard Manley Hopkins was a Jesuit priest whose poetry was not recognized while he was alive. In fact, although he died in 1889, his works were not published until 1918 and only began to be recognized in 1930.

1) Who is the persona in this poem?

    A) A woman
    B) An old man
    C) A farmer
    D) The poet, himself, a priest
    E) A villager

The correct answer is D:) The poet, himself, a priest.

2) Hopkins' philosophy emphasized the individuality of every natural thing, which he called "inscape." In the following items, select the one that *does not* reflect that philosophy.

    A) Whatever is fickle, freckled
    B) All the trades
    C) All things counter
    D) swift, slow; sweet, sour; adazzle, dim
    E) Praise him

The correct answer is E:) Praise him.

3) He also initiated a new form of rhythm for his poetry, which he called "sprung"rhythm. It is measured by feet of from one to four syllables with any number of weak syllables. Contrary to the iambs (_/) of the poems by Frost and Dickenson, the stress is on the first syllable in "sprung" rhythm. The rhythm of the first two lines is as follows:

In what way does this conform to the characteristics of "sprung" rhythm?

    A) It has iambs (_/).
    B) It has six feet.
    C) The first syllable is stressed.
    D) There are three stresses at the beginning.
    E) The second line begins with an unstressed syllable.

The correct answer is C:) The first syllable is stressed.

4) Hopkins' poetry is characterized by the strong images it suggests. What is a couple-colour sky?

    A) A blue sky.
    B) A cloudy sky.
    C) A stormy sky.
    D) A blue sky with many small bits of white clouds.
    E) A grey sky.

The correct answer is D:) A blue sky with many small bits of white clouds.

5) What does a brinded cow suggest?

    A) A Holstein
    B) A black cow
    C) A cow with a coat of two colors mixed together
    D) A white cow
    E) A brown cow

The correct answer is C:) A cow with a coat of two colors mixed together.

6) What does "He fathers-forth whose beauty is past change" mean?

    A) His father is handsome.
    B) God is love.
    C) God makes all things.
    D) God's creation is diverse and it is beautiful.
    E) His father has beautiful children.

The correct answer is D:) God's creation is diverse and it is beautiful.

7) Alliteration is the repetition of a sound. Which of the following is an example of alliteration?

    A) Fathers-forth
    B) Beauty is past change
    C) Dappled things
    D) Brinded cow
    E) Beauty is past change

The correct answer is A:) Fathers-forth.

8) Select the example of alliteration from the following:

    A) Swift, slow; sweet, sour
    B) Chestnut-falls
    C) Finches' wings
    D) Counter, original, spare
    E) Rose-moles all in stipple

The correct answer is A:) Swift, slow; sweet, sour.

Poem #4
The Magi
William Butler Yeats (1865-1939)

Now as at all times I can see in the mind's eye,
In their stiff, painted clothes, the pale unsatisfied ones
Appear and disappear in the blue depth of the sky
With all their ancient faces like rain-beaten stones,
And all their helms of silver hovering side by side,
And all their eyes still fixed, hoping to find once more,
Being by Calvary's turbulence unsatisfied,
The uncontrollable mystery on the bestial floor.

1) William Butler Yeats was an Irish poet who believed that prophesies had been
    revealed to him. He believed that the world goes in two-thousand-year cycles and
    that the Christian cycle would come to an end in the year 2000. He saw it as an
    ever-widening gyre with everything gradually coming apart and anarchy being
    loosed on the world. As the gyre widens, "things fall apart; the center cannot
    hold," he believed. Where in "The Magi" is that theme found?

    A) I can see in the mind's eye
    B) The pale unsatisfied ones
    C) helms of silver
    D) Being by Calvary's turbulence unsatisfied
    E) the blue depth of the sky

The correct answer is D:) Being by Calvary's turbulence unsatisfied.

2) The rhythm in this poem is extremely irregular.
The first two lines:

How does this very irregular rhythm enforce the theme?

    A) It is appropriate to a jarring theme.
    B) It doesn't enforce the theme.
    C) It provides a contrast to the theme of the Magi.
    D) It is not relevant to the theme.
    E) It makes the reading of it interesting.

The correct answer is A:) It is appropriate to a jarring theme.

3) What does the image of "Calvary's turbulence unsatisfied" suggest?

    A) That there will be another crucifixion.
    B) That the salvation bought by the crucifixion will no longer be sufficient.
    C) That there will be another virgin birth.
    D) That Calvary brought turbulence on the earth.
    E) That Christianity has brought unrest in the world.

The correct answer is B:) That the salvation bought by the crucifixion will no longer be sufficient.

4) What does "the pale unsatisfied ones" refer to?

    A) The three kings (the Magi) who brought gifts to the baby Jesus
    B) Christians who are no longer committed to their faith
    C) Non-Christians
    D) Devout Christians
    E) Leaders of the modern world

The correct answer is A:) The three kings (the Magi) who brought gifts to the baby Jesus.

5) What does the bestial floor refer to?

   A) The anarchy to come
   B) People will behave like animals
   C) The birth of Jesus in a manger
   D) The widening gyre
   E) Conditions in the modern world

The correct answer is C:) The birth of Jesus in a manger.

Poem #5
Sonnet #60
William Shakespeare (1564-1616)

Like as the waves make toward the pebbled shore,
So do our minutes hasten to their end;
Each changing place with that which goes before,
In sequent toil all forwards do contend.
Nativity, once in the main (*broad expanse*) of light,
Crawls to maturity, wherewith being crowned,
Crooked eclipses 'gainst his glory fight,
And time that gave doth now his gift confound.
Time doth transfix the flourish (*remove the embellishment*) set on youth
And delves the parallels in beauty's brow,
Feeds on the rarities of nature's truth,
And nothing stands but for his scythe to mow.
And yet to times in hope (*future times*) my verse shall stand,
Praising thy worth, despite his cruel hand.

(Note: the italicized phrases in parentheses are translations of the phrase preceding.)

William Shakespeare is best known for his plays; however, he wrote a number of sonnets like #60. They were not published in his lifetime. It appears that he wrote them for his friends and not for publication.

1) What is the theme of Sonnet #60?

    A) Passage of time.
    B) The effects of the passage of time on a human being.
    C) Poems will endure even after the poet is dead.
    D) Time is the enemy of youth.
    E) Growing old is depressing.

The correct answer is B:) The effects of the passage of time on a human being.

2) Who is the persona?

    A) A lover who is growing older
    B) An old man
    C) A young man
    D) A woman
    E) A young lover

The correct answer is A:) A lover who is growing older.

3) To whom is he/she speaking?

    A) No one in particular
    B) A lover who is growing older
    C) His/her children
    D) His/her friends
    E) His family

The correct answer is B:) A lover who is growing older.

4) What simile (direct comparison) can you find in this sonnet?

    A) "Like as the waves make towards the pebbled shore, so do our minutes hasten to their end;"
    B) "In sequent toil all forwards do contend"
    C) "And time that gave doth now his gift confound."
    D) "yet to times in hope my verse shall stand."
    E) "feeds on the rarities of nature's truth."

The correct answer is A:) "Like as the waves make towards the pebbled shore, so do our minutes hasten to their end;"

5) What metaphor (implied comparison) can you find?

    A) "In sequent toil all forwards do contend."
    B) "And nothing stands but for his scythe to mow."
    C) "Time doth transfix the flourish set on youth"
    D) "Each changing place with that which goes before."
    E) "In sequent toil all forwards do contend."

The correct answer is B:) "And nothing stands but for his scythe to mow."

6) The rhythm is a consistent iambic pentameter (5 feet of iambs-- _ /). However, there are two lines where this rhythm is broken. In the following, what is the line where the rhythm is not iambic pentameter?

    A) Line 1
    B) Line 13
    C) Line 6
    D) Line 7
    E) Line 2

The correct answer is C:) Line 6.

Authors and Their Works

1) In Greek mythology, who was said to have brought fire to mankind?

    A) Athena
    B) Hercules
    C) Prometheus
    D) Hermes
    E) Hades

The correct answer is C:) Prometheus. Due to a trick of Prometheus, the precedent was set that fat and bones, rather than the more useful and preferable meat, should be sacrificed to the Gods. Zeus was angered by the trickery of Prometheus and withheld fire from mankind. However, Prometheus once again helped mankind by stealing some fire and introducing it to mortals.

2) In which medieval work is the search for Truth the central plot?

   A) *The Faerie Queen*
   B) *Prometheus*
   C) *Piers Plowman*
   D) *Everyman*
   E) Both A and C

The correct answer is C:) *Piers Plowman*. The poem is highly allegorical and written in alliterative verse. It tells the story of a character named Will who has a series of visions through which he searches for Truth (a figurative person symbolic of ultimate truth in the real world).

3) In which of the following was Queen Elizabeth the inspiration for the fictional character Queen Gloriana?

   A) *The Faerie Queen*
   B) *Everyman*
   C) *Piers Plowman*
   D) *Prometheus*
   E) *Canterbury Tales*

The correct answer is A:) *The Faerie Queen*. One of Spenser's motives in writing the poem was as a compliment the monarch Queen Elizabeth, and it boldly claims a connection between her linage and that of King Arthur. Queen Elizabeth is equated with the Faerie Queen Gloriana.

4) Thomas Carlyle, John Stuart Mills and John Ruskin were all know for what type of writings?

   A) Victorian
   B) Enlightenment
   C) Raphaelite
   D) Romantic
   E) None of the above

The correct answer is D:) Romantic. The Romantic Period of literature began in Europe in the 18th century and was prevalent throughout the 19th century. The movement was largely a reaction against the Enlightenment ideals, and shifted focus from science and reason, to individuality, nature, and emotion.

5) The periodical *The Germ* was founded by which movement?

    A) Enlightenment
    B) Victorian
    C) Humanist
    D) Romantic
    E) Pre-Raphaelite

The correct answer is E:) Pre-Raphaelite. Followers of pre-Raphaelite philosophy were very descriptive, sensual, and detail oriented in their writing as well. A periodical known as *The Germ* was even founded during this time, although it published only four editions. The brotherhood was initially founded by William Holman Hunt, John Everett Millais, and Dante Gabriel Rossetti.

6) Which of the following BEST describes a picaresque?

    A) A fable meant to articulate important social ideals
    B) An early form of novel portraying a rogue character surviving through deception and trickery
    C) A social commentary extolling the high morality of society
    D) Poetry designed to invoke feelings of deep emotion within the reader
    E) None of the above

The correct answer is B:) An early form of novel portraying a rogue character surviving through deception and trickery. A picaresque novel was an early form of novel that takes its name from Spanish origins. It derives from a word meaning rogue or rascal. The central plot of a picaresque is a depiction of a low-born, roguish character as they go about their life and attempt to survive.

7) In Greek mythology, Prometheus was a

    A) Titan
    B) Demigod
    C) God
    D) Mortal
    E) Satyr

The correct answer is A:) Titan. Prometheus was a Greek Titan known for his trickery and cunning.

8) In Charles Lamb's famous letter to Wordsworth, he

   A) Graciously accepted an offer to visit his home
   B) Ridiculed his style of writing as archaic
   C) Praised his writing as innovative and evocative
   D) Declined an offer to collaborate in producing a poetic work
   E) Criticized the idea of country life, and declined an offer to visit

The correct answer is E:) Criticized the idea of country life, and declined an offer to visit. Although the two corresponded often and were friends, in the letter Lamb offered satiric criticism of Wordsworth's country lifestyle. Rather, Lamb praises the constantly changing life of the city.

9) Which of the following uses personification of Death to express faith in resurrection?

   A) *Miller's Tale*
   B) *Death Be Not Proud*
   C) *Everyman*
   D) *An Artist's Studio*
   E) *Between Two Worlds*

The correct answer is B:) *Death Be Not Proud.* In the poem, John Donne uses personification of death by claiming that death is slave to men. Further, he concludes with the exclamation with death itself will one day die.

10) The *Reeve's Tale* and the *Miller's Tale* are

   A) Romantic novels
   B) Petrarchan sonnets
   C) Moral poems
   D) Fabliaux
   E) None of the above

The correct answer is D:) Fabliaux. The fabliaux was a style of writing initially popularized in France in the 12th century, but which spread in small measure to England and other parts of Europe. The fabliaux were sarcastic, cynical, and comic stories, usually in poetic verse.

11) Which of the following is a work of Matthew Arnold?

    A) Stanzas from the *Great Chartreuse*
    B) *An Artist's Studio*
    C) *Richard Cory*
    D) *Everyman*
    E) *Death Be Not Proud*

The correct answer is A:) Stanzas from the *Great Chartreuse*. One of his most famous passages is from a long poem entitled Stanzas from the Great Chartreuse. The Great Chartreuse was a castle that Arnold visited, and the poem was written while he was there.

12) What is the central theme of the medieval play Everyman?

    A) Virtues such as patience and love must be sought for diligently
    B) Grace is the foundation of salvation in the afterlife
    C) All but your good deeds will abandon you in the end
    D) The rightful king will always rule in the end
    E) None of the above

The correct answer is C:) All but your good deeds will abandon you in the end. As Everyman proceeds on his journey to death, he seeks to bring others along with him – discretion, knowledge, confession, strength, beauty, and kindred – but all abandon him in the end. As he goes to his grave, only Good Deeds remains with Everyman. The message of the play is a warning that all but good deeds will abandon every man in the end.

13) Which author claims that their work is speculative fiction?

    A) Matthew Arnold
    B) Christina Rossetti
    C) William Wordsworth
    D) John Donne
    E) Margaret Atwood

The correct answer is E:) Margaret Atwood. Margaret Atwood is a renowned Canadian author and poet. She prefers the designation of speculative fiction, claiming that there is a difference between writing about things that can't happen, science fiction, and things that haven't happened, speculative fiction.

14) Who is known for pulling a sword free from stone?

    A) Merlin
    B) King Arthur
    C) Sir Galahad
    D) Lancelot
    E) Uther Pendragon

The correct answer is B:) King Arthur. The most famous story in Arthurian lore is that of the young Arthur accidentally pulling the sword free from stone. The act earned him his rightful place as king.

15) The first American dictionary was written by

    A) Samuel Johnson
    B) Merriam Webster
    C) John Donne
    D) Richard Cory
    E) William Wordsworth

The correct answer is A:) Samuel Johnson. Prior to Johnson there was no consistency to the written English language.

16) Christina Rossetti's poem "In An Artist's Studio" describes a studio in which

    A) Only the color blue is used
    B) All the artwork features the same woman
    C) A person has recently died
    D) The artist is metaphorically compared to King Arthur
    E) None of the above

The correct answer is B:) All the artwork features the same woman. The poem describes an artist's studio which is filled with work, but notes that each piece reflects the same female subject. The poem implies that this has the effect of imprisoning the woman. Rather than freeing her, she becomes a slave to the perceptions of the artist.

17) In the poem "Richard Cory" by Edwin Arlington Robinson, what happens to Richard Cory?

    A) He inherits great wealth
    B) He makes new friends
    C) He kills himself
    D) He falls off a bridge
    E) He shares his wealth with the town

The correct answer is C:) He kills himself. Through the poem, Robinson shows that wealth does not bring happiness, and that human companionship is far more important to a successful life. Although Richard Cory may have appeared to have everything in life – he was clean, healthy, and a gentleman – in truth he was not happy at all. In the end, he shoots himself.

 # Test-Taking Strategies

Here are some test-taking strategies that are specific to this test and to other CLEP tests in general:

- Keep your eyes on the time. Pay attention to how much time you have left.
- Read the entire question and read all the answers. Many questions are not as hard to answer as they may seem. Sometimes, a difficult sounding question really only is asking you how to read an accompanying chart. Chart and graph questions are on most CLEP tests and should be an easy free point.
- If you don't know the answer immediately, the new computer-based testing lets you mark questions and come back to them later if you have time.
- Read the wording carefully. Some words can give you hints to the right answer. There are no exceptions to an answer when there are words in the question such as always, all or none. If one of the answer choices includes most or some of the right answers, but not all, then that is not the correct answer. Here is an example:

    The primary colors include all of the following:

        A) Red, Yellow, Blue, Green
        B) Red, Green, Yellow
        C) Red, Orange, Yellow
        D) Red, Yellow, Blue
        E) None of the above

Although item A includes all the right answers, it also includes an incorrect answer, making it incorrect. If you didn't read it carefully, were in a hurry, or didn't know the material well, you might fall for this.

- Make a guess on a question that you do not know the answer to. There is no penalty for an incorrect answer. Eliminate the answer choices that you know are incorrect. For example, this will let your guess be a 1 in 3 chance instead.

 # What Your Score Means

Based on your score, you may, or may not, qualify for credit at your specific institution. At University of Phoenix, a score of 50 is passing for full credit. At Utah Valley University, the score is unpublished, the school will accept credit on a case-by-case basis. Another school, Brigham Young University (BYU) does not accept CLEP credit. To find out what score you need for credit, you need to get that information from your school's website or academic advisor.

You can score between 20 and 80 on any CLEP test. Some exams include percentile ranks. Each correct answer is worth one point. You lose no points for unanswered or incorrect questions.

 # Test Preparation

How much you need to study depends on your knowledge of a subject area. If you are interested in literature, took it in school, or enjoy reading then your studying and preparation for the literature or humanities test will not need to be as intensive as someone who is new to literature.

This book is much different than the regular CLEP study guides. This book actually teaches you the information that you need to know to pass the test. If you are particularly interested in an area, or feel like you want more information, do a quick search online. There is a lot you'll need to memorize. Almost everything in this book will be on the test. It is important to understand all major theories and concepts listed in the table of contents. It is also very important to know any bolded words.

Don't worry if you do not understand or know a lot about the area. If you study hard, you can complete and pass the test.

To prepare for the test, make a series of goals. Allot a certain amount of time to review the information you have already studied and to learn additional material. Take notes as you study-it will help you learn the material.

 # Legal Note

 # Appendix

THE SHORT HAPPY LIFE OF FRANCIS MACOMBER - A SHORT STORY BY ERNEST HEMINGWAY

can be read online at: http://www.tarleton.edu/Faculty/sword/Short%20Story/The%20Short%20Happy%20Life%20of%20Francis%20Macomber.pdf

THE FALL OF THE HOUSE OF USHER - A SHORT STORY BY EDGAR ALLAN POE

DURING the whole of a dull, dark, and soundless day in the autumn of the year, when the clouds hung oppressively low in the heavens, I had been passing alone, on horse-back, through a singularly dreary tract of country ; and at length found myself, as the shades of the evening drew on, within view of the melancholy House of Usher. I know not how it was - but, with the first glimpse of the building, a sense of insufferable gloom pervaded my spirit. I say insufferable ; for the feeling was unrelieved by any of that half-pleasurable, because poetic, sentiment, with which the mind usually receives even the sternest natural images of the desolate or terrible. I looked upon the scene before me - upon the mere house, and the simple landscape features of the domain - upon the bleak walls - upon the vacant eye-like windows - upon a few rank sedges - and upon a few white trunks of decayed trees - with an utter depression of soul which I can compare to no earthly sensation more properly than to the after-dream of the reveller upon opium - the bitter lapse into everyday life - the hideous dropping off of the veil. There was an iciness, a sinking, a sickening of the heart - an unredeemed dreariness of thought which no goading of the imagination could torture into aught of the sublime. What was it - I paused to think - what was it that so unnerved me in the contemplation of the House of Usher ? It was a mystery all insoluble ; nor could I grapple with the shadowy fancies that crowded upon me as I pondered. I was forced to fall back upon the unsatisfactory conclusion, that while, beyond doubt, there are combinations of very simple natural objects which have the power of thus affecting us, still the analysis of this power lies among considerations beyond our depth. It was possible, I reflected, that a mere different arrangement of the particulars of the scene, of the details of the picture, would be sufficient to modify, or perhaps to annihilate its capacity for sorrowful impression ; and, acting upon this idea, I reined my horse to the precipitous brink of a black and lurid tarn that lay in unruffled lustre by the dwelling, and gazed down - but with a shudder even more thrilling than before - upon the remodelled and inverted images of the gray sedge, and the ghastly tree-stems, and the vacant and eye-like windows.

Nevertheless, in this mansion of gloom I now proposed to myself a sojourn of some weeks. Its proprietor, Roderick Usher, had been one of my boon companions in boyhood ; but many years had elapsed since our last meeting. A letter, however, had lately reached me in a distant part of the country - a letter from him - which, in its wildly importunate nature, had admitted of no other than a personal reply. The MS. gave evidence of nervous agitation. The writer spoke of acute bodily illness - of a mental disorder which oppressed him - and of an earnest desire to see me, as his best, and indeed his only personal friend, with a view of attempting, by the cheerfulness of my society, some alleviation of his malady. It was the manner in which all this, and much more, was said - it was the apparent heart that went with his request - which allowed me no room for hesitation; and I accordingly obeyed forthwith what I still considered a very singular summons.

Although, as boys, we had been even intimate associates, yet I really knew little of my friend. His reserve had been always excessive and habitual. I was aware, however, that his very ancient family had been noted, time out of mind, for a peculiar sensibility of temperament, displaying itself, through long ages, in many works of exalted art, and manifested, of late, in repeated deeds of munificent yet unobtrusive charity, as well as in a passionate devotion to the intricacies, perhaps even more than to the orthodox and easily recognisable beauties, of musical science. I had learned, too, the very remarkable fact, that the stem of the Usher race, all time-honored as it was, had put forth, at no period, any enduring branch ; in other words, that the entire family lay in the direct line of descent, and had always, with very trifling and very temporary variation, so lain. It was this deficiency, I considered, while running over in thought the perfect keeping of the character of the premises with the accredited character of the people, and while speculating upon the possible influence which the one, in the long lapse of centuries, might have exercised upon the other - it was this deficiency, perhaps, of collateral issue, and the consequent undeviating transmission, from sire to son, of the patrimony with the name, which had, at length, so identified the two as to merge the original title of the estate in the quaint and equivocal appellation of the "House of Usher" - an appellation which seemed to include, in the minds of the peasantry who used it, both the family and the family mansion.

I have said that the sole effect of my somewhat childish experiment - that of looking down within the tarn - had been to deepen the first singular impression. There can be no doubt that the consciousness of the rapid increase of my superstition - for why should I not so term it ? - served mainly to accelerate the increase itself. Such, I have long known, is the paradoxical law of all sentiments having terror as a basis. And it might have been for this reason only, that, when I again uplifted my eyes to the house itself, from its image in the pool, there grew in my mind a strange fancy - a fancy so ridiculous, indeed, that I but mention it to show the vivid force of the sensations which oppressed me. I had so worked upon my imagination as really to believe that about the whole mansion and domain there hung an atmosphere peculiar to themselves and their immediate vicinity - an atmosphere which had no affinity with the air of heaven, but which had reeked up from the decayed trees, and the gray wall, and the silent tarn - a pestilent and mystic vapor, dull, sluggish, faintly discernible, and leaden-hued.

Shaking off from my spirit what must have been a dream, I scanned more narrowly the real aspect of the building. Its principal feature seemed to be that of an excessive antiquity. The discoloration of ages had been great. Minute fungi overspread the whole exterior, hanging in a fine tangled web-work from the eaves. Yet all this was apart from any extraordinary dilapidation. No portion of the masonry had fallen ; and there appeared to be a wild inconsistency between its still perfect adaptation of parts, and the crumbling condition of the individual stones. In this there was much that reminded me of the specious totality of old wood-work which has rotted for long years in some neglected vault, with no disturbance from the breath of the external air. Beyond this in-dication of extensive decay, however, the fabric gave little token of instability. Perhaps the eye of a scrutinizing observer might have discovered a barely perceptible fissure, which, extending from the roof of the building in front, made its way down the wall in a zigzag direction, until it became lost in the sullen waters of the tarn.

Noticing these things, I rode over a short causeway to the house. A servant in waiting took my horse, and I entered the Gothic archway of the hall. A valet, of stealthy step, thence conducted me, in silence, through many dark and intricate passages in my prog-ress to the studio of his master. Much that I encountered on the way contributed, I know not how, to heighten the vague sentiments of which I have already spoken. While the objects around me - while the carvings of the ceilings, the sombre tapestries of the walls, the ebon blackness of the floors, and the phantasmagoric armorial trophies which rattled as I strode, were but matters to which, or to such as which, I had been accus-tomed from my infancy - while I hesitated not to acknowledge how familiar was all this - I still wondered to find how unfamiliar were the fancies which ordinary images were stirring up. On one of the staircases, I met the physician of the family. His countenance,

I thought, wore a mingled expression of low cunning and perplexity. He accosted me with trepidation and passed on. The valet now threw open a door and ushered me into the presence of his master.

The room in which I found myself was very large and lofty. The windows were long, narrow, and pointed, and at so vast a distance from the black oaken floor as to be altogether inaccessible from within. Feeble gleams of encrimsoned light made their way through the trellissed panes, and served to render sufficiently distinct the more prominent objects around ; the eye, however, struggled in vain to reach the remoter angles of the chamber, or the recesses of the vaulted and fretted ceiling. Dark draperies hung upon the walls. The general furniture was profuse, comfortless, antique, and tattered. Many books and musical instruments lay scattered about, but failed to give any vitality to the scene. I felt that I breathed an atmosphere of sorrow. An air of stern, deep, and irredeemable gloom hung over and pervaded all.

Upon my entrance, Usher arose from a sofa on which he had been lying at full length, and greeted me with a vivacious warmth which had much in it, I at first thought, of an overdone cordiality - of the constrained effort of the ennuyé ; man of the world. A glance, however, at his countenance, convinced me of his perfect sincerity. We sat down ; and for some moments, while he spoke not, I gazed upon him with a feeling half of pity, half of awe. Surely, man had never before so terribly altered, in so brief a period, as had Roderick Usher ! It was with difficulty that I could bring myself to admit the identity of the wan being before me with the companion of my early boyhood. Yet the character of his face had been at all times remarkable. A cadaverousness of complexion ; an eye large, liquid, and luminous beyond comparison ; lips somewhat thin and very pallid, but of a surpassingly beautiful curve ; a nose of a delicate Hebrew model, but with a breadth of nostril unusual in similar formations ; a finely moulded chin, speaking, in its want of prominence, of a want of moral energy; hair of a more than web-like softness and tenuity ; these features, with an inordinate expansion above the regions of the temple, made up altogether a countenance not easily to be forgotten. And now in the mere exaggeration of the prevailing character of these features, and of the expression they were wont to convey, lay so much of change that I doubted to whom I spoke. The now ghastly pallor of the skin, and the now miraculous lustre of the eye, above all things startled and even awed me. The silken hair, too, had been suffered to grow all unheeded, and as, in its wild gossamer texture, it floated rather than fell about the face, I could not, even with effort, connect its Arabesque expression with any idea of simple humanity.

In the manner of my friend I was at once struck with an incoherence - an inconsistency ; and I soon found this to arise from a series of feeble and futile struggles to overcome an habitual trepidancy - an excessive nervous agitation. For something of this nature I had indeed been prepared, no less by his letter, than by reminiscences of certain boyish traits, and by conclusions deduced from his peculiar physical conformation and temperament. His action was alternately vivacious and sullen. His voice varied rapidly from a tremulous indecision (when the animal spirits seemed utterly in abeyance) to that species of energetic concision - that abrupt, weighty, unhurried, and hollow-sounding enunciation - that leaden, self-balanced and perfectly modulated guttural utterance, which may be observed in the lost drunkard, or the irreclaimable eater of opium, during the periods of his most intense excitement.

It was thus that he spoke of the object of my visit, of his earnest desire to see me, and of the solace he expected me to afford him. He entered, at some length, into what he conceived to be the nature of his malady. It was, he said, a constitutional and a family evil, and one for which he despaired to find a remedy - a mere nervous affection, he immediately added, which would undoubtedly soon pass off. It displayed itself in a host of unnatural sensations. Some of these, as he detailed them, interested and bewildered me ; although, perhaps, the terms, and the general manner of the narration had their weight. He suffered much from a morbid acuteness of the senses ; the most insipid food was alone endurable; he could wear only garments of certain texture ; the odors of all flowers were oppressive ; his eyes were tortured by even a faint light ; and there were but peculiar sounds, and these from stringed instruments, which did not inspire him with horror.

To an anomalous species of terror I found him a bounden slave. "I shall perish," said he, "I must perish in this deplorable folly. Thus, thus, and not otherwise, shall I be lost. I dread the events of the future, not in themselves, but in their results. I shudder at the thought of any, even the most trivial, incident, which may operate upon this intolerable agitation of soul. I have, indeed, no abhorrence of danger, except in its absolute effect - in terror. In this unnerved - in this pitiable condition - I feel that the period will sooner or later arrive when I must abandon life and reason together, in some struggle with the grim phantasm, FEAR."

I learned, moreover, at intervals, and through broken and equivocal hints, another singular feature of his mental condition. He was enchained by certain superstitious impressions in regard to the dwelling which he tenanted, and whence, for many years, he had never ventured forth - in regard to an influence whose supposititious force was conveyed in terms too shadowy here to be re-stated - an influence which some peculiarities in the mere form and substance of his family mansion, had, by dint of long sufferance, he said, obtained over his spirit - an effect which the physique of the gray walls and turrets, and of the dim tarn into which they all looked down, had, at length, brought about upon the morale of his existence.

He admitted, however, although with hesitation, that much of the peculiar gloom which thus afflicted him could be traced to a more natural and far more palpable origin - to the severe and long-continued illness - indeed to the evidently approaching dissolution - of a tenderly beloved sister - his sole companion for long years - his last and only relative on earth. "Her decease," he said, with a bitterness which I can never forget, "would leave him (him the hopeless and the frail) the last of the ancient race of the Ushers." While he spoke, the lady Madeline (for so was she called) passed slowly through a remote portion of the apartment, and, without having noticed my presence, disappeared. I regarded her with an utter astonishment not unmingled with dread - and yet I found it impossible to account for such feelings. A sensation of stupor oppressed me, as my eyes followed her retreating steps. When a door, at length, closed upon her, my glance sought instinctively and eagerly the countenance of the brother - but he had buried his face in his hands, and I could only perceive that a far more than ordinary wanness had overspread the emaciated fingers through which trickled many passionate tears.

The disease of the lady Madeline had long baffled the skill of her physicians. A settled apathy, a gradual wasting away of the person, and frequent although transient affections of a partially cataleptical character, were the unusual diagnosis. Hitherto she had steadily borne up against the pressure of her malady, and had not betaken herself finally to bed ; but, on the closing in of the evening of my arrival at the house, she succumbed (as her brother told me at night with inexpressible agitation) to the prostrating power of the destroyer ; and I learned that the glimpse I had obtained of her person would thus probably be the last I should obtain - that the lady, at least while living, would be seen by me no more.

For several days ensuing, her name was unmentioned by either Usher or myself: and during this period I was busied in earnest endeavors to alleviate the melancholy of my friend. We painted and read together ; or I listened, as if in a dream, to the wild improvisations of his speaking guitar. And thus, as a closer and still closer intimacy admitted me more unreservedly into the recesses of his spirit, the more bitterly did I perceive the futility of all attempt at cheering a mind from which darkness, as if an inherent positive quality, poured forth upon all objects of the moral and physical universe, in one unceasing radiation of gloom.

I shall ever bear about me a memory of the many solemn hours I thus spent alone with the master of the House of Usher. Yet I should fail in any attempt to convey an idea of the exact character of the studies, or of the occupations, in which he involved me, or led me the way. An excited and highly distempered ideality threw a sulphureous lustre over all. His long improvised dirges will ring forever in my ears. Among other things, I hold painfully in mind a certain singular perversion and amplification of the wild air of the last waltz of Von Weber. From the paintings over which his elaborate fancy brooded, and which grew, touch by touch, into vaguenesses at which I shuddered the more thrillingly, because I shuddered knowing not why ; - from these paintings (vivid as their images now are before me) I would in vain endeavor to educe more than a small portion which should lie within the compass of merely written words. By the utter simplicity, by the nakedness of his designs, he arrested and overawed attention. If ever mortal painted an idea, that mortal was Roderick Usher. For me at least - in the circumstances then surrounding me - there arose out of the pure abstractions which the hypochondriac contrived to throw upon his canvass, an intensity of intolerable awe, no shadow of which felt I ever yet in the contemplation of the certainly glowing yet too concrete reveries of Fuseli.

One of the phantasmagoric conceptions of my friend, partaking not so rigidly of the spirit of abstraction, may be shadowed forth, although feebly, in words. A small picture presented the interior of an immensely long and rectangular vault or tunnel, with low walls, smooth, white, and without interruption or device. Certain accessory points of the design served well to convey the idea that this excavation lay at an exceeding depth below the surface of the earth. No outlet was observed in any portion of its vast extent, and no torch, or other artificial source of light was discernible ; yet a flood of intense rays rolled throughout, and bathed the whole in a ghastly and inappropriate splendor.

I have just spoken of that morbid condition of the auditory nerve which rendered all music intolerable to the sufferer, with the exception of certain effects of stringed in-struments. It was, perhaps, the narrow limits to which he thus confined himself upon the guitar, which gave birth, in great measure, to the fantastic character of his perfor-mances. But the fervid facility of his impromptus could not be so accounted for. They must have been, and were, in the notes, as well as in the words of his wild fantasias (for he not unfrequently accompanied himself with rhymed verbal improvisations), the result of that intense mental collectedness and concentration to which I have previously alluded as observable only in particular moments of the highest artificial excitement. The words of one of these rhapsodies I have easily remembered. I was, perhaps, the more forcibly impressed with it, as he gave it, because, in the under or mystic current of its meaning, I fancied that I perceived, and for the first time, a full consciousness on the part of Usher, of the tottering of his lofty reason upon her throne. The verses, which were entitled "The Haunted Palace," ran very nearly, if not accurately, thus:
I.
In the greenest of our valleys,
By good angels tenanted,
Once a fair and stately palace -
Radiant palace - reared its head.
In the monarch Thought's dominion -
It stood there !
Never seraph spread a pinion
Over fabric half so fair.
II.
Banners yellow, glorious, golden,
On its roof did float and flow;
(This - all this - was in the olden
Time long ago)
And every gentle air that dallied,

In that sweet day,
Along the ramparts plumed and pallid,
A winged odor went away.
III.
Wanderers in that happy valley
Through two luminous windows saw
Spirits moving musically
To a lute's well-tunéd law,
Round about a throne, where sitting
(Porphyrogene !)
In state his glory well befitting,
The ruler of the realm was seen.
IV.
And all with pearl and ruby glowing
Was the fair palace door,
Through which came flowing, flowing, flowing,
And sparkling evermore,
A troop of Echoes whose sweet duty
Was but to sing,
In voices of surpassing beauty,
The wit and wisdom of their king.
V.
But evil things, in robes of sorrow,
Assailed the monarch's high estate ;
(Ah, let us mourn, for never morrow
Shall dawn upon him, desolate !)
And, round about his home, the glory
That blushed and bloomed
Is but a dim-remembered story
Of the old time entombed.
VI.
And travellers now within that valley,
Through the red-litten windows, see
Vast forms that move fantastically
To a discordant melody ;
While, like a rapid ghastly river,
Through the pale door,
A hideous throng rush out forever,
And laugh - but smile no more.

I well remember that suggestions arising from this ballad, led us into a train of thought wherein there became manifest an opinion of Usher's which I mention not so much on account of its novelty, (for other men have thought thus,) as on account of the pertinacity with which he maintained it. This opinion, in its general form, was that of the sentience of all vegetable things. But, in his disordered fancy, the idea had assumed a more daring character, and trespassed, under certain conditions, upon the kingdom of inorganization. I lack words to express the full extent, or the earnest abandon of his persuasion. The belief, however, was connected (as I have previously hinted) with the gray stones of the home of his forefathers. The conditions of the sentience had been here, he imagined, fulfilled in the method of collocation of these stones - in the order of their arrangement, as well as in that of the many fungi which overspread them, and of the decayed trees which stood around - above all, in the long undisturbed endurance of this arrangement, and in its reduplication in the still waters of the tarn. Its evidence - the evidence of the sentience - was to be seen, he said, (and I here started as he spoke,) in the gradual yet certain condensation of an atmosphere of their own about the waters and the walls. The result was discoverable, he added, in that silent, yet importunate and terrible influence which for centuries had moulded the destinies of his family, and which made him what I now saw him - what he was. Such opinions need no comment, and I will make none.

Our books - the books which, for years, had formed no small portion of the mental existence of the invalid - were, as might be supposed, in strict keeping with this character of phantasm. We pored together over such works as the Ververt et Chartreuse of Gresset ; the Belphegor of Machiavelli ; the Heaven and Hell of Swedenborg ; the Subterranean Voyage of Nicholas Klimm by Holberg ; the Chiromancy of Robert Flud, of Jean D'Indaginé, and of De la Chambre ; the Journey into the Blue Distance of Tieck ; and the City of the Sun of Campanella. One favorite volume was a small octavo edition of the Directorium Inquisitorium , by the Dominican Eymeric de Gironne; and there were passages in Pomponius Mela, about the old African Satyrs and Oegipans, over which Usher would sit dreaming for hours. His chief delight, however, was found in the perusal of an exceedingly rare and curious book in quarto Gothic - the manual of a forgotten church - the Vigiliae Mortuorum secundum Chorum Ecclesiae Maguntinae .

I could not help thinking of the wild ritual of this work, and of its probable influence upon the hypochondriac, when, one evening, having informed me abruptly that the lady Madeline was no more, he stated his intention of preserving her corpse for a fortnight, (previously to its final interment,) in one of the numerous vaults within the main walls of the building. The worldly reason, however, assigned for this singular proceeding, was one which I did not feel at liberty to dispute. The brother had been led to his resolution (so he told me) by consideration of the unusual character of the malady of the deceased, of certain obtrusive and eager inquiries on the part of her medical men, and of the remote and exposed situation of the burial-ground of the family. I will not deny that when I called to mind the sinister countenance of the person whom I met upon the staircase, on the day of my arrival at the house, I had no desire to oppose what I regarded as at best but a harmless, and by no means an unnatural, precaution.

At the request of Usher, I personally aided him in the arrangements for the temporary entombment. The body having been encoffined, we two alone bore it to its rest. The vault in which we placed it (and which had been so long unopened that our torches, half smothered in its oppressive atmosphere, gave us little opportunity for investigation) was small, damp, and entirely without means of admission for light ; lying, at great depth, immediately beneath that portion of the building in which was my own sleeping apartment. It had been used, apparently, in remote feudal times, for the worst purposes of a donjon-keep, and, in later days, as a place of deposit for powder, or some other highly combustible substance, as a portion of its floor, and the whole interior of a long archway through which we reached it, were carefully sheathed with copper. The door, of massive iron, had been, also, similarly protected. Its immense weight caused an unusually sharp grating sound, as it moved upon its hinges.

Having deposited our mournful burden upon tressels within this region of horror, we partially turned aside the yet unscrewed lid of the coffin, and looked upon the face of the tenant. A striking similitude between the brother and sister now first arrested my attention ; and Usher, divining, perhaps, my thoughts, murmured out some few words from which I learned that the deceased and himself had been twins, and that sympathies of a scarcely intelligible nature had always existed between them. Our glances, however, rested not long upon the dead - for we could not regard her unawed. The disease which had thus entombed the lady in the maturity of youth, had left, as usual in all maladies of a strictly cataleptical character, the mockery of a faint blush upon the bosom and the face, and that suspiciously lingering smile upon the lip which is so terrible in death. We replaced and screwed down the lid, and, having secured the door of iron, made our way, with toil, into the scarcely less gloomy apartments of the upper portion of the house.

And now, some days of bitter grief having elapsed, an observable change came over the features of the mental disorder of my friend. His ordinary manner had vanished. His ordinary occupations were neglected or forgotten. He roamed from chamber to chamber with hurried, unequal, and objectless step. The pallor of his countenance had assumed, if possible, a more ghastly hue - but the luminousness of his eye had utterly gone out. The once occasional huskiness of his tone was heard no more; and a tremulous quaver, as if of extreme terror, habitually characterized his utterance. There were times, indeed, when I thought his unceasingly agitated mind was laboring with some oppressive secret, to divulge which he struggled for the necessary courage. At times, again, I was obliged to resolve all into the mere inexplicable vagaries of madness, for I beheld him gazing upon vacancy for long hours, in an attitude of the profoundest attention, as if listening to some imaginary sound. It was no wonder that his condition terrified - that it infected me. I felt creeping upon me, by slow yet certain degrees, the wild influences of his own fantastic yet impressive superstitions.

It was, especially, upon retiring to bed late in the night of the seventh or eighth day after the placing of the lady Madeline within the donjon, that I experienced the full power of such feelings. Sleep came not near my couch - while the hours waned and waned away. I struggled to reason off the nervousness which had dominion over me. I endeavored to believe that much, if not all of what I felt, was due to the bewildering influence of the gloomy furniture of the room - of the dark and tattered draperies, which, tortured into motion by the breath of a rising tempest, swayed fitfully to and fro upon the walls, and rustled uneasily about the decorations of the bed. But my efforts were fruitless. An irrepressible tremor gradually pervaded my frame ; and, at length, there sat upon my very heart an incubus of utterly causeless alarm. Shaking this off with a gasp and a struggle, I uplifted myself upon the pillows, and, peering earnestly within the intense darkness of the chamber, harkened - I know not why, except that an instinctive spirit prompted me - to certain low and indefinite sounds which came, through the pauses of the storm, at long intervals, I knew not whence. Overpowered by an intense sentiment of horror, unaccountable yet unendurable, I threw on my clothes with haste (for I felt that I should sleep no more during the night), and endeavored to arouse myself from the pitiable condition into which I had fallen, by pacing rapidly to and fro through the apartment.

I had taken but few turns in this manner, when a light step on an adjoining staircase arrested my attention. I presently recognised it as that of Usher. In an instant afterward he rapped, with a gentle touch, at my door, and entered, bearing a lamp. His countenance was, as usual, cadaverously wan - but, moreover, there was a species of mad hilarity in his eyes - an evidently restrained hysteria in his whole demeanor. His air appalled me - but anything was preferable to the solitude which I had so long endured, and I even welcomed his presence as a relief.

"And you have not seen it ?" he said abruptly, after having stared about him for some moments in silence - "you have not then seen it ? - but, stay ! you shall." Thus speaking, and having carefully shaded his lamp, he hurried to one of the casements, and threw it freely open to the storm.

The impetuous fury of the entering gust nearly lifted us from our feet. It was, indeed, a tempestuous yet sternly beautiful night, and one wildly singular in its terror and its beauty. A whirlwind had apparently collected its force in our vicinity ; for there were frequent and violent alterations in the direction of the wind ; and the exceeding density of the clouds (which hung so low as to press upon the turrets of the house) did not prevent our perceiving the life-like velocity with which they flew careering from all points against each other, without passing away into the distance. I say that even their exceeding density did not prevent our perceiving this - yet we had no glimpse of the moon or stars - nor was there any flashing forth of the lightning. But the under surfaces of the huge masses of agitated vapor, as well as all terrestrial objects immediately around us, were glowing in the unnatural light of a faintly luminous and distinctly visible gaseous exhalation which hung about and enshrouded the mansion.

"You must not - you shall not behold this !" said I, shudderingly, to Usher, as I led him, with a gentle violence, from the window to a seat. "These appearances, which bewilder you, are merely electrical phenomena not uncommon - or it may be that they have their ghastly origin in the rank miasma of the tarn. Let us close this casement ; - the air is chilling and dangerous to your frame. Here is one of your favorite romances. I will read, and you shall listen ; - and so we will pass away this terrible night together."

The antique volume which I had taken up was the "Mad Trist" of Sir Launcelot Canning ; but I had called it a favorite of Usher's more in sad jest than in earnest ; for, in truth, there is little in its uncouth and unimaginative prolixity which could have had interest for the lofty and spiritual ideality of my friend. It was, however, the only book immediately at hand ; and I indulged a vague hope that the excitement which now agitated the hypochondriac, might find relief (for the history of mental disorder is full of similar anomalies) even in the extremeness of the folly which I should read. Could I have judged, indeed, by the wild overstrained air of vivacity with which he harkened, or apparently harkened, to the words of the tale, I might well have congratulated myself upon the success of my design.

I had arrived at that well-known portion of the story where Ethelred, the hero of the Trist, having sought in vain for peaceable admission into the dwelling of the hermit, proceeds to make good an entrance by force. Here, it will be remembered, the words of the narrative run thus:

"And Ethelred, who was by nature of a doughty heart, and who was now mighty withal, on account of the powerfulness of the wine which he had drunken, waited no longer to hold parley with the hermit, who, in sooth, was of an obstinate and maliceful turn, but, feeling the rain upon his shoulders, and fearing the rising of the tempest, uplifted his mace outright, and, with blows, made quickly room in the plankings of the door for his gauntleted hand ; and now pulling therewith sturdily, he so cracked, and ripped, and tore all asunder, that the noise of the dry and hollow-sounding wood alarummed and reverberated throughout the forest."

At the termination of this sentence I started, and for a moment, paused ; for it appeared to me (although I at once concluded that my excited fancy had deceived me) - it appeared to me that, from some very remote portion of the mansion, there came, indistinctly, to my ears, what might have been, in its exact similarity of character, the echo (but a stifled and dull one certainly) of the very cracking and ripping sound which Sir Launcelot had so particularly described. It was, beyond doubt, the coincidence alone which had arrested my attention ; for, amid the rattling of the sashes of the casements, and the ordinary commingled noises of the still increasing storm, the sound, in itself, had nothing, surely, which should have interested or disturbed me. I continued the story:

"But the good champion Ethelred, now entering within the door, was sore enraged and amazed to perceive no signal of the maliceful hermit ; but, in the stead thereof, a dragon of a scaly and prodigious demeanor, and of a fiery tongue, which sate in guard before a palace of gold, with a floor of silver ; and upon the wall there hung a shield of shining brass with this legend enwritten -

Who entereth herein, a conqueror hath bin ;
Who slayeth the dragon, the shield he shall win;

And Ethelred uplifted his mace, and struck upon the head of the dragon, which fell before him, and gave up his pesty breath, with a shriek so horrid and harsh, and withal so piercing, that Ethelred had fain to close his ears with his hands against the dreadful noise of it, the like whereof was never before heard."

Here again I paused abruptly, and now with a feeling of wild amazement - for there could be no doubt whatever that, in this instance, I did actually hear (although from what direction it proceeded I found it impossible to say) a low and apparently distant, but harsh, protracted, and most unusual screaming or grating sound - the exact counterpart of what my fancy had already conjured up for the dragon's unnatural shriek as described by the romancer.

Oppressed, as I certainly was, upon the occurrence of this second and most extraordinary coincidence, by a thousand conflicting sensations, in which wonder and extreme terror were predominant, I still retained sufficient presence of mind to avoid exciting, by any observation, the sensitive nervousness of my companion. I was by no means certain that he had noticed the sounds in question ; although, assuredly, a strange alteration had, during the last few minutes, taken place in his demeanor. From a position fronting my own, he had gradually brought round his chair, so as to sit with his face to the door of the chamber ; and thus I could but partially perceive his features, although I saw that his lips trembled as if he were murmuring inaudibly. His head had dropped upon his breast - yet I knew that he was not asleep, from the wide and rigid opening of the eye as I caught a glance of it in profile. The motion of his body, too, was at variance with this idea - for he rocked from side to side with a gentle yet constant and uniform sway. Having rapidly taken notice of all this, I resumed the narrative of Sir Launcelot, which thus proceeded:

"And now, the champion, having escaped from the terrible fury of the dragon, bethinking himself of the brazen shield, and of the breaking up of the enchantment which was upon it, removed the carcass from out of the way before him, and approached valorously over the silver pavement of the castle to where the shield was upon the wall ; which in sooth tarried not for his full coming, but fell down at his feet upon the silver floor, with a mighty great and terrible ringing sound."

No sooner had these syllables passed my lips, than - as if a shield of brass had indeed, at the moment, fallen heavily upon a floor of silver - I became aware of a distinct, hollow, metallic, and clangorous, yet apparently muffled reverberation. Completely unnerved, I leaped to my feet ; but the measured rocking movement of Usher was undisturbed. I rushed to the chair in which he sat. His eyes were bent fixedly before him, and throughout his whole countenance there reigned a stony rigidity. But, as I placed my hand upon his shoulder, there came a strong shudder over his whole person ; a sickly smile quivered about his lips ; and I saw that he spoke in a low, hurried, and gibbering murmur, as if unconscious of my presence. Bending closely over him, I at length drank in the hideous import of his words.

"Not hear it ? - yes, I hear it, and have heard it. Long - long - long - many minutes, many hours, many days, have I heard it - yet I dared not - oh, pity me, miserable wretch that I am ! - I dared not - I dared not speak ! We have put her living in the tomb ! Said I not that my senses were acute ? I now tell you that I heard her first feeble movements in the hollow coffin. I heard them - many, many days ago - yet I dared not - I dared not speak ! And now - to-night - Ethelred - ha ! ha ! - the breaking of the hermit's door, and the death-cry of the dragon, and the clangor of the shield ! - say, rather, the rending of her coffin, and the grating of the iron hinges of her prison, and her struggles within the coppered archway of the vault ! Oh whither shall I fly ? Will she not be here anon ? Is she not hurrying to upbraid me for my haste ? Have I not heard her footstep on the stair ? Do I not distinguish that heavy and horrible beating of her heart ? Madman !" - here he sprang furiously to his feet, and shrieked out his syllables, as if in the effort he were giving up his soul - " Madman ! I tell you that she now stands without the door ! "

As if in the superhuman energy of his utterance there had been found the potency of a spell - the huge antique pannels to which the speaker pointed, threw slowly back, upon the instant, their ponderous and ebony jaws. It was the work of the rushing gust - but then without those doors there did stand the lofty and enshrouded figure of the lady Madeline of Usher. There was blood upon her white robes, and the evidence of some bitter struggle upon every portion of her emaciated frame. For a moment she remained trembling and reeling to and fro upon the threshold - then, with a low moaning cry, fell heavily inward upon the person of her brother, and in her violent and now final death-agonies, bore him to the floor a corpse, and a victim to the terrors he had anticipated.

From that chamber, and from that mansion, I fled aghast. The storm was still abroad in all its wrath as I found myself crossing the old causeway. Suddenly there shot along the path a wild light, and I turned to see whence a gleam so unusual could have issued ; for the vast house and its shadows were alone behind me. The radiance was that of the full, setting, and blood-red moon, which now shone vividly through that once barely-discernible fissure, of which I have before spoken as extending from the roof of the building, in a zigzag direction, to the base. While I gazed, this fissure rapidly widened - there came a fierce breath of the whirlwind - the entire orb of the satellite burst at once upon my sight - my brain reeled as I saw the mighty walls rushing asunder - there was a long tumultuous shouting sound like the voice of a thousand waters - and the deep and dank tarn at my feet closed sullenly and silently over the fragments of the "House of Usher ."

THE REAL THING - A SHORT STORY BY HENRY JAMES

CHAPTER I

When the porter's wife, who used to answer the house-bell, announced "A gentleman and a lady, sir," I had, as I often had in those days--the wish being father to the thought--an immediate vision of sitters. Sitters my visitors in this case proved to be; but not in the sense I should have preferred. There was nothing at first however to indicate that they mightn't have come for a portrait. The gentleman, a man of fifty, very high and very straight, with a moustache slightly grizzled and a dark grey walking-coat admirably fitted, both of which I noted professionally--I don't mean as a barber or yet as a tailor--would have struck me as a celebrity if celebrities often were striking. It was a truth of which I had for some time been conscious that a figure with a good deal of frontage was, as one might say, almost never a public institution. A glance at the lady helped to remind me of this paradoxical law: she also looked too distinguished to be a "personality." Moreover one would scarcely come across two variations together.

Neither of the pair immediately spoke--they only prolonged the preliminary gaze suggesting that each wished to give the other a chance. They were visibly shy; they stood there letting me take them in--which, as I afterwards perceived, was the most practical thing they could have done. In this way their embarrassment served their cause. I had seen people painfully reluctant to mention that they desired anything so gross as to be represented on canvas; but the scruples of my new friends appeared almost insurmountable. Yet the gentleman might have said "I should like a portrait of my wife," and the lady might have said "I should like a portrait of my husband." Perhaps they weren't husband and wife--this naturally would make the matter more delicate. Perhaps they wished to be done together--in which case they ought to have brought a third person to break the news.

"We come from Mr. Rivet," the lady finally said with a dim smile that had the effect of a moist sponge passed over a "sunk" piece of painting, as well as of a vague allusion to vanished beauty. She was as tall and straight, in her degree, as her companion, and with ten years less to carry. She looked as sad as a woman could look whose face was not charged with expression; that is her tinted oval mask showed waste as an exposed surface shows friction. The hand of time had played over her freely, but to an effect of elimination. She was slim and stiff, and so well-dressed, in dark blue cloth, with lappets and pockets and buttons, that it was clear she employed the same tailor as her husband. The couple had an indefinable air of prosperous thrift--they evidently got a good deal of luxury for their money. If I was to be one of their luxuries it would behove me to consider my terms.

"Ah Claude Rivet recommended me?" I echoed and I added that it was very kind of him, though I could reflect that, as he only painted landscape, this wasn't a sacrifice.

The lady looked very hard at the gentleman, and the gentleman looked round the room. Then staring at the floor a moment and stroking his moustache, he rested his pleasant eyes on me with the remark: "He said you were the right one."

"I try to be, when people want to sit."

"Yes, we should like to," said the lady anxiously.

"Do you mean together?"

My visitors exchanged a glance. "If you could do anything with ME I suppose it would be double," the gentleman stammered.

"Oh yes, there's naturally a higher charge for two figures than for one."

"We should like to make it pay," the husband confessed.

"That's very good of you," I returned, appreciating so unwonted a sympathy--for I supposed he meant pay the artist.

A sense of strangeness seemed to dawn on the lady. "We mean for the illustrations--Mr. Rivet said you might put one in."

"Put in--an illustration?" I was equally confused.

"Sketch her off, you know," said the gentleman, colouring.

It was only then that I understood the service Claude Rivet had rendered me; he had told them how I worked in black-and-white, for magazines, for story-books, for sketches of contemporary life, and consequently had copious employment for models. These things were true, but it was not less true--I may confess it now; whether because the aspiration was to lead to everything or to nothing I leave the reader to guess--that I couldn't get the honours, to say nothing of the emoluments, of a great painter of portraits out of my head. My "illustrations" were my pot-boilers; I looked to a different branch of art--far and away the most interesting it had always seemed to me--to perpetuate my fame.

There was no shame in looking to it also to make my fortune but that fortune was by so much further from being made from the moment my visitors wished to be "done" for nothing. I was disappointed; for in the pictorial sense I had immediately SEEN them. I had seized their type--I had already settled what I would do with it. Something that wouldn't absolutely have pleased them, I afterwards reflected.

"Ah you're--you're--a -?" I began as soon as I had mastered my surprise. I couldn't bring out the dingy word "models": it seemed so little to fit the case.

"We haven't had much practice," said the lady.

"We've got to do something, and we've thought that an artist in your line might perhaps make something of us," her husband threw off. He further mentioned that they didn't know many artists and that they had gone first, on the off-chance--he painted views of course, but sometimes put in figures; perhaps I remembered--to Mr. Rivet, whom they had met a few years before at a place in Norfolk where he was sketching.

"We used to sketch a little ourselves," the lady hinted.

"It's very awkward, but we absolutely must do something," her husband went on.

"Of course we're not so VERY young," she admitted with a wan smile.

With the remark that I might as well know something more about them the husband had handed me a card extracted from a neat new pocket- book--their appurtenances were all of the freshest--and inscribed with the words "Major Monarch." Impressive as these words were they didn't carry my knowledge much further; but my visitor presently added: "I've left the army and we've had the misfortune to lose our money. In fact our means are dreadfully small."

"It's awfully trying--a regular strain,", said Mrs. Monarch.

They evidently wished to be discreet--to take care not to swagger because they were gentlefolk. I felt them willing to recognise this as something of a drawback, at the same time that I guessed at an underlying sense--their consolation in adversity--that they HAD their points. They certainly had; but these advantages struck me as preponderantly social; such for instance as would help to make a drawing-room look well. However, a drawing-room was always, or ought to be, a picture.

In consequence of his wife's allusion to their age Major Monarch observed: "Naturally it's more for the figure that we thought of going in. We can still hold ourselves up." On the instant I saw that the figure was indeed their strong point. His "naturally" didn't sound vain, but it lighted up the question. "SHE has the best one," he continued, nodding at his wife with a pleasant after- dinner absence of circumlocution. I could only reply, as if we were in fact sitting over our wine, that this didn't prevent his own from being very good; which led him in turn to make answer: "We thought that if you ever have to do people like us we might be something like it. SHE particularly--for a lady in a book, you know."

I was so amused by them that, to get more of it, I did my best to take their point of view; and though it was an embarrassment to find myself appraising physically, as if they were animals on hire or useful blacks, a pair whom I should have expected to meet only in one of the relations in which criticism is tacit, I looked at Mrs. Monarch judicially enough to be able to exclaim after a moment with conviction: "Oh yes, a lady in a book!" She was singularly like a bad illustration.

"We'll stand up, if you like," said the Major; and he raised himself before me with a really grand air.

I could take his measure at a glance--he was six feet two and a perfect gentleman. It would have paid any club in process of formation and in want of a stamp to engage him at a salary to stand in the principal window. What struck me at once was that in coming to me they had rather missed their vocation; they could surely have been turned to better account for advertising purposes. I couldn't of course see the thing in detail, but I could see them make somebody's fortune--I don't mean their own. There was something in them for a waistcoat-maker, an hotel-keeper or a soap-vendor. I could imagine "We always use it" pinned on their bosoms with the greatest effect; I had a vision of the brilliancy with which they would launch a table d'hote.

Mrs. Monarch sat still, not from pride but from shyness, and presently her husband said to her: "Get up, my dear, and show how smart you are." She obeyed, but she had no need to get up to show it. She walked to the end of the studio and then came back blushing, her fluttered eyes on the partner of her appeal. I was reminded of an incident I had accidentally had a glimpse of in Paris--being with a friend there, a dramatist about to produce a play, when an actress came to him to ask to be entrusted with a part. She went through her paces before him, walked up and down as Mrs. Monarch was doing. Mrs. Monarch did it quite as well, but I abstained from applauding. It was very odd to see such people apply for such poor pay. She looked as if she had ten thousand a year. Her husband had used the word that described her: she was in the London current jargon essentially and typically "smart." Her figure was, in the same order of ideas, conspicuously and irreproachably "good." For a woman of her age her waist was surprisingly small; her elbow moreover had the orthodox crook. She held her head at the conventional angle, but why did she come to ME? She ought to have tried on jackets at a big shop. I feared my visitors were not only destitute but "artistic"--which would be a great complication. When she sat down again I thanked her, observing that what a draughtsman most valued in his model was the faculty of keeping quiet.

"Oh SHE can keep quiet," said Major Monarch. Then he added jocosely: "I've always kept her quiet."

"I'm not a nasty fidget, am I?" It was going to wring tears from me, I felt, the way she hid her head, ostrich-like, in the other broad bosom.

The owner of this expanse addressed his answer to me. "Perhaps it isn't out of place to mention--because we ought to be quite business-like, oughtn't we?--that when I married her she was known as the Beautiful Statue."

"Oh dear!" said Mrs. Monarch ruefully.

"Of course I should want a certain amount of expression," I rejoined.

"Of COURSE!"--and I had never heard such unanimity.

"And then I suppose you know that you'll get awfully tired."

"Oh we NEVER get tired!" they eagerly cried.

"Have you had any kind of practice?"

They hesitated--they looked at each other. We've been photographed--IMMENSELY," said Mrs. Monarch.

"She means the fellows have asked us themselves," added the Major.

"I see--because you're so good-looking."

"I don't know what they thought, but they were always after us."

"We always got our photographs for nothing,"

smiled Mrs. Monarch.

"We might have brought some, my dear," her husband remarked.

"I'm not sure we have any left. We've given quantities away," she explained to me.

"With our autographs and that sort of thing," said the Major.

"Are they to be got in the shops?" I inquired as a harmless pleasantry.

"Oh yes, HERS--they used to be."

"Not now," said Mrs. Monarch with her eyes on the floor.

CHAPTER II

I could fancy the "sort of thing" they put on the presentation copies of their photographs, and I was sure they wrote a beautiful hand. It was odd how quickly I was sure of everything that concerned them. If they were now so poor as to have to cam shillings and pence they could never have had much of a margin. Their good looks had been their capital, and they had good- humouredly made the most of the career that this resource marked out for them. It was in their faces, the blankness, the deep intellectual repose of the twenty years of country-house visiting that had given them pleasant intonations. I could see the sunny drawing-rooms, sprinkled with periodicals she didn't read, in which Mrs. Monarch had continuously sat; I could see the wet shrubberies in which she had walked, equipped to admiration for either exercise. I could see the rich covers the Major had helped to shoot and the wonderful garments in which, late at night, he repaired to the smoking-room to talk about them. I could imagine their leggings and waterproofs, their knowing tweeds and rugs, their rolls of sticks and cases of tackle and neat umbrellas; and I could evoke the exact appearance of their servants and the compact variety of their luggage on the platforms of country stations.

They gave small tips, but they were liked; they didn't do anything themselves, but they were welcome. They looked so well everywhere; they gratified the general relish for stature, complexion and "form." They knew it without fatuity or vulgarity, and they respected themselves in consequence. They weren't superficial: they were thorough and kept themselves up--it had been their line. People with such a taste for activity had to have some line. I could feel how even in a dull house they could have been counted on for the joy of life. At present something had happened--it didn't matter what, their little income had grown less, it had grown least--and they had to do something for pocket-money. Their friends could like them, I made out, without liking to support them. There was something about them that represented credit-- their clothes, their manners, their type; but if credit is a large empty pocket in which an occasional chink reverberates, the chink at least must be audible. What they wanted of me was help to make it so. Fortunately they had no children--I soon divined that. They would also perhaps wish our relations to be kept secret: this was why it was "for the figure"--the reproduction of the face would betray them.

I liked them--I felt, quite as their friends must have done--they were so simple; and I had no objection to them if they would suit. But somehow with all their perfections I didn't easily believe in them. After all they were amateurs, and the ruling passion of my life was--the detestation of the amateur. Combined with this was another perversity--an innate preference for the represented subject over the real one: the defect of the real one was so apt to be a lack of representation. I liked things that appeared; then one was sure. Whether they WERE or not was a subordinate and almost always a profitless question. There were other considerations, the first of which was that I already had two or three recruits in use, notably a young person with big feet, in alpaca, from Kilburn, who for a couple of years had come to me regularly for my illustrations and with whom I was still--perhaps ignobly--satisfied. I frankly explained to my visitors how the case stood, but they had taken more precautions than I supposed. They had reasoned out their opportunity, for Claude Rivet had told them of the projected edition de luxe of one of the writers of our day--the rarest of the novelists--who, long neglected by the multitudinous vulgar, and dearly prized by the attentive (need I mention Philip Vincent?) had had the happy fortune of seeing, late in life, the dawn and then the full light of a higher criticism; an estimate in which on the part of the public there was something really of expiation. The edition preparing, planned by a publisher of taste, was practically an act of high reparation; the woodcuts with which it was to be enriched were the homage of English art to one of the most independent representatives of English letters. Major and Mrs. Monarch confessed to me they had hoped I might be able to work THEM into my branch of the enterprise. They knew I was to do the first of the books, Rutland Ramsay, but I had to make clear to them that my participation in the rest of the affair--this first book was to be a test--must depend on the satisfaction I should give. If this should be limited my employers would drop me with scarce common forms. It was therefore a crisis for me, and naturally I was making special preparations, looking about for new people, should they be necessary, and securing the best types. I admitted however that I should like to settle down to two or three good models who would do for everything.

"Should we have often to--a--put on special clothes?" Mrs. Monarch timidly demanded.

"Dear yes--that's half the business."

"And should we be expected to supply our own costumes?

"Oh no; I've got a lot of things. A painter's models put on--or put off--anything he likes."

"And you mean--a--the same?"

"The same?"

Mrs. Monarch looked at her husband again.

"Oh she was just wondering," he explained, "if the costumes are in GENERAL use." I had to confess that they were, and I mentioned further that some of them--I had a lot of, genuine greasy last- century things--had served their time, a hundred years ago, on living world-stained men and women; on figures not perhaps so far removed, in that vanished world, from THEIR type, the Monarchs', quoi! of a breeched and bewigged age. "We'll put, on anything that FITS," said the Major.

"Oh I arrange that--they fit in the pictures."

"I'm afraid I should do better for the modern books. I'd come as you like," said Mrs. Monarch.

"She has got a lot of clothes at home: they might do for contemporary life," her husband continued.

"Oh I can fancy scenes in which you'd be quite natural." And indeed I could see the slipshod re-arrangements of stale properties--the stories I tried to produce pictures for without the exasperation of reading them--whose sandy tracts the good lady might help to people. But I had to return to the fact that--for this sort of work--the daily mechanical grind--I was already equipped: the people I was working with wore fully adequate.

"We only thought we might be more like SOME characters," said Mrs. Monarch mildly, getting up.

Her husband also rose; he stood looking at me with a dim wistfulness that was touching in so fine a man. "Wouldn't it be rather a pull sometimes to have--a--to haven?" He hung fire; he wanted me to help him by phrasing what he meant. But I couldn't--I didn't know. So he brought it out awkwardly: "The REAL thing; a gentleman, you know, or a lady." I was quite ready to give a general assent--I admitted that there was a great deal in that. This encouraged Major Monarch to say, following up his appeal with an unacted gulp: "It's awfully hard--we've tried everything." The gulp was communicative; it proved too much for his wife. Before I knew it Mrs. Monarch had dropped again upon a divan and burst into tears. Her husband sat down beside her, holding one of her hands; whereupon she quickly dried her eyes with the other, while I felt embarrassed as she looked up at me. "There isn't a confounded job I haven't applied for--waited for--prayed for. You can fancy we'd be pretty bad first. Secretaryships and that sort of thing? You might as well ask for a peerage. I'd be ANYTHING--I'm strong; a messenger or a coalheaver. I'd put on a gold-laced cap and open carriage-doors in front of the haberdasher's; I'd hang about a station to carry portmanteaux; I'd be a postman. But they won't LOOK at you; there are thousands as good as yourself already on the ground. GENTLEMEN, poor beggars, who've drunk their wine, who've kept their hunters!"

I was as reassuring as I knew how to be, and my visitors were presently on their feet again while, for the experiment, we agreed on an hour. We were discussing it when the door opened and Miss Churm came in with a wet umbrella. Miss Churm had to take the omnibus to Maida Vale and then walk half a mile. She looked a trifle blowsy and slightly splashed. I scarcely ever saw her come in without thinking afresh how odd it was that, being so little in herself, she should yet be so much in others. She was a meagre little Miss Churm, but was such an ample heroine of romance. She was only a freckled cockney, but she could represent everything, from a fine lady to a shepherdess, she had the faculty as she might have had a fine voice or long hair. She couldn't spell and she loved beer, but she had two or three "points," and practice, and a knack, and mother-wit, and a whimsical sensibility, and a love of the theatre, and seven sisters,--and not an ounce of respect, especially for the H. The first thing my visitors saw was that her umbrella was wet, and in their spotless perfection they visibly winced at it. The rain had come on since their arrival.

"I'm all in a soak; there WAS a mess of people in the 'bus. I wish you lived near a stytion," said Miss Churm. I requested her to get ready as quickly as possible, and she passed into the room in which she always changed her dress. But before going out she asked me what she was to get into this time.

"It's the Russian princess, don't you know?" I answered; "the one with the 'golden eyes,' in black velvet, for the long thing in the Cheapside."

"Golden eyes? I SAY!" cried Miss Churm, while my companions watched her with intensity as she withdrew. She always arranged herself, when she was late, before I could turn round; and I kept my visitors a little on purpose, so that they might get an idea, from seeing her, what would be expected of themselves. I mentioned that she was quite my notion of ail excellent model--she was really very clever.

"Do you think she looks like a Russian princess?" Major Monarch asked with lurking alarm.

"When I make her, yes."

"Oh if you have to MAKE her--!" he reasoned, not without point.

"That's the most you can ask. There are so many who are not makeable."

"Well now, HERE'S a lady"--and with a persuasive smile he passed his arm into his wife's--"who's already made!"

"Oh I'm not a Russian princess," Mrs. Monarch protested a little coldly. I could see she had known some and didn't like them. There at once was a complication of a kind I never had to fear with Miss Churm.

This young lady came back in black velvet--the gown was rather rusty and very low on her lean shoulders--and with a Japanese fan in her red hands. I reminded her that in the scene I was doing she had to look over some one's head. "I forget whose it is but it doesn't matter. Just look over a head."

"I'd rather look over a stove," said Miss Churm and she took her station near the fire. She fell into Position, settled herself into a tall attitude, gave a certain backward inclination to her head and a certain forward droop to her fan, and looked, at least to my prejudiced sense, distinguished and charming, foreign and dangerous. We left her looking so while I went downstairs with Major and Mrs. Monarch.

"I believe I could come about as near it as that," said Mrs. Monarch.

"Oh you think she's shabby, but you must allow for the alchemy of art."

However, they went off with an evident increase of comfort founded on their demonstrable advantage in being the real thing. I could fancy them shuddering over Miss Churm. She was very droll about them when I went back, for I told her what they wanted.

"Well, if SHE can sit I'll tyke to bookkeeping," said my model.

"She's very ladylike," I replied as an innocent form of aggravation.

"So much the worse for YOU. That means she can't turn round."

"She'll do for the fashionable novels."

"Oh yes, she'll DO for them!" my model humorously declared. "Ain't they bad enough without her?" I had often sociably denounced them to Miss Churm.

CHAPTER III

It was for the elucidation of a mystery in one of these works that I first tried Mrs. Monarch. Her husband came with her, to be useful if necessary--it was sufficiently clear that as a general thing he would prefer to come with her. At first I wondered if this were for "propriety's" sake--if he were going to be jealous and meddling. The idea was too tiresome, and if it had been confirmed it would speedily have brought our acquaintance to a close. But I soon saw there was nothing in it and that if he accompanied Mrs. Monarch it was--in addition to the chance of being wanted--simply because he had nothing else to do. When they were separate his occupation was gone, and they never

HAD been separate. I judged rightly that in their awkward situation their close union was their main comfort and that this union had no weak spot. It was a real marriage, an encouragement to the hesitating, a nut for pessimists to crack. Their address was humble--I remember afterwards thinking it had been the only thing about them that was really professional--and I could fancy the lamentable lodgings in which the Major would have been left alone. He could sit there more or less grimly with his wife--he couldn't sit there anyhow without her.

He had too much tact to try and make himself agreeable when he couldn't be useful; so when I was too absorbed in my work to talk he simply sat and waited. But I liked to hear him talk--it made my work, when not interrupting it, less mechanical, less special. To listen to him was to combine the excitement of going out with the economy of staying at home. There was only one hindrance--that I seemed not to know any of the people this brilliant couple had known. I think he wondered extremely, during the term of our intercourse, whom the deuce I DID know. He hadn't a stray sixpence of an idea to fumble for, so we didn't spin it very fine; we confined ourselves to questions of leather and even of liquor- saddlers and breeches-makers and how to get excellent claret cheap- -and matters like "good trains" and the habits of small game. His lore on these last subjects was astonishing--he managed to interweave the station-master with the ornithologist. When he couldn't talk about greater things he could talk cheerfully about smaller, and since I couldn't accompany him into reminiscences of the fashionable world he could lower the conversation without a visible effort to my level.

So earnest a desire to please was touching in a man who could so easily have knocked one down. He looked after the fire and had an opinion on the draught of the stove without my asking him, and I could see that he thought many of my arrangements not half knowing. I remember telling him that if I were only rich I'd offer him a salary to come and teach me how to live. Sometimes he gave a random sigh of which the essence might have been: "Give me even such a bare old-barrack as this, and I'd do something with it!" When I wanted to use him he came alone; which was an illustration of the superior courage of women. His wife could bear her solitary second floor, and she was in general more discreet; showing by various small reserves that she was alive to the propriety of keeping our relations markedly professional--not letting them slide into sociability. She wished it to remain clear that she and the Major were employed, not cultivated, and if she approved of me as a superior, who could be kept in his place, she never thought me quite good enough for an equal.

She sat with great intensity, giving the whole of her mind to it, and was capable of remaining for an hour almost as motionless as before a photographer's lens. I could see she had been photographed often, but somehow the very habit that made her good for that purpose unfitted her for mine. At first I was extremely pleased with her ladylike air, and it was a satisfaction, on coming to follow her lines, to see how good they were and how far they could lead the pencil. But after a little skirmishing I began to find her too insurmountably stiff; do what I would with it my drawing looked like a photograph or a copy of a photograph. Her figure had no variety of expression--she herself had no sense of variety. You may say that this was my business and was only a question of placing her. Yet I placed her in every conceivable position and she managed to obliterate their differences. She was always a lady certainly, and into the bargain was always the same lady. She was the real thing, but always the same thing. There were moments when I rather writhed under the serenity of her confidence that she WAS the real thing. All her dealings with me and all her husband's were an implication that this was lucky for ME. Meanwhile I found myself trying to invent types that approached her own, instead of making her own transform itself--in the clever way that was not impossible for instance to poor Miss Churm. Arrange as I would and take the precautions I would, she always came out, in my pictures, too tall--landing me in the dilemma of having represented a fascinating woman as seven feet high, which (out of respect perhaps to my own very much scantier inches) was far from my idea of such a personage.

The case was worse with the Major--nothing I could do would keep HIM down, so that he became useful only for the representation of brawny giants. I adored variety and range, I cherished human accidents, the illustrative note; I wanted to characterise closely, and the thing in the world I most hated was the danger of being ridden by a type. I had quarrelled with some of my friends about it; I had parted company with them for maintaining that one HAD to be, and that if the type was beautiful--witness Raphael and Leonardo--the servitude was only a gain. I was neither Leonardo nor Raphael--I might only be a presumptuous young modern searcher; but I held that everything was to be sacrificed sooner than character. When they claimed that the obsessional form could easily BE character I retorted, perhaps superficially, "Whose?" It couldn't be everybody's--it might end in being nobody's.

After I had drawn Mrs. Monarch a dozen times I felt surer even than before that the value of such a model as Miss Churm resided precisely in the fact that she had no positive stamp, combined of course with the other fact that what she did have was a curious and inexplicable talent for imitation. Her usual appearance was like a curtain which--she could draw up at request for a capital performance. This performance was simply suggestive; but it was a word to the wise--it was vivid and pretty. Sometimes even I thought it, though she was plain herself, too insipidly pretty; I made it a reproach to her that the figures drawn from her were monotonously (betement, as we used to say) graceful. Nothing made her more angry: it was so much her pride to feel she could sit for characters that had nothing in common with each other. She would accuse me at such moments of taking away her "reputytion."

It suffered a certain shrinkage, this queer quantity, from the repeated visits of my new friends. Miss Churm was greatly in demand, never in want of employment, so I had no scruple in putting her off occasionally, to try them more at my ease. It was certainly amusing at first to do the real thing--it was amusing to do Major Monarch's trousers.

They WERE the real thing, even if he did come out colossal. It was amusing to do his wife's back hair-- it was so mathematically neat--and the particular "smart" tension of her tight stays. She lent herself especially to positions in which the face was somewhat averted or blurred, she abounded in ladylike back views and profils perdus. When she stood erect she took naturally one of the attitudes in which court-painters represent queens and princesses; so that I found myself wondering whether, to draw out this accomplishment, I couldn't get the editor of the Cheapside to publish a really royal romance, "A Tale of Buckingham Palace." Sometimes however the real thing and the make- believe came into contact; by which I mean that Miss Churm, keeping an appointment or coming to make one on days when I had much work in hand, encountered her invidious rivals. The encounter was not on their part, for they noticed her no more than if she had been the housemaid; not from intentional loftiness, but simply because as yet, professionally, they didn't know how to fraternise, as I could imagine they would have liked--or at least that the Major would. They couldn't talk about the omnibus--they always walked; and they didn't know what else to try--she wasn't interested in good trains or cheap claret. Besides, they must have felt--in the air--that she was amused at them, secretly derisive of their ever knowing how. She wasn't a person to conceal the limits of her faith if she had had a chance to show them. On the other hand Mrs. Monarch didn't think her tidy; for why else did she take pains to say to me--it was going out of the way, for Mrs. Monarch--that she didn't like dirty women?

One day when my young lady happened to be present with my other sitters--she even dropped in, when it was convenient, for a chat--I asked her to be so good as to lend a hand in getting tea, a service with which she was familiar and which was one of a class that, living as I did in a small way, with slender domestic resources, I often appealed to my models to render. They liked to lay hands on my property, to break the sitting, and sometimes the china--it made them feel Bohemian. The next time I saw Miss Churm after this incident she surprised me greatly by making a scene about it--she accused me of having wished to humiliate her. She hadn't resented the outrage at the time, but had seemed obliging and amused, enjoying the comedy of asking Mrs. Monarch, who sat vague and silent, whether she would have cream and sugar, and putting an exaggerated simper into the question. She had tried intonations-- as if she too wished to pass for the real thing--till I was afraid my other visitors would take offence.

Oh they were determined not to do this, and their touching patience was the measure of their great need. They would sit by the hour, uncomplaining, till I was ready to use them; they would come back on the chance of being wanted and would walk away cheerfully if it failed. I used to go to the door with them to see in what magnificent order they retreated. I tried to find other employment for them--I introduced them to several artists. But they didn't "take," for reasons I could appreciate, and I became rather anxiously aware that after such disappointments they fell back upon me with a heavier weight. They did me the honour to think me most their form. They weren't romantic enough for the painters, and in those days there were few serious workers in black-and-white.

Besides, they had an eye to the great job I had mentioned to them-- they had secretly set their hearts on supplying the right essence for my pictorial vindication of our fine novelist. They knew that for this undertaking I should want no costume--effects, none of the frippery of past ages--that it was a case in which everything would be contemporary and satirical and presumably genteel. If I could work them into it their future would be assured, for the labour would of course be long and the occupation steady.

One day Mrs. Monarch came without her husband--she explained his absence by his having had to go to the City. While she sat there in her usual relaxed majesty there came at the door a knock which I immediately recognised as the subdued appeal of a model out of work. It was followed by the entrance of a young man whom I at once saw to be a foreigner and who proved in fact an Italian acquainted with no English word but my name, which he uttered in a way that made it seem to include all others. I hadn't then visited his country, nor was I proficient in his tongue; but as he was not so meanly constituted--what Italian is?--as to depend only on that member for expression he conveyed to me, in familiar but graceful mimicry, that he was in search of exactly the employment in which the lady before me was engaged. I was not struck with him at first, and while I continued to draw I dropped few signs of interest or encouragement. He stood his ground however--not importunately, but with a dumb dog-like fidelity in his eyes that amounted to innocent impudence, the manner of a devoted servant--he might have been in the house for years--unjustly suspected. Suddenly it struck me that this very attitude and expression made a picture; whereupon I told him to sit down and wait till I should be free. There was another picture in the way he obeyed me, and I observed as I worked that there were others still in the way he looked wonderingly, with his head thrown back, about the high studio. He might have been crossing himself in Saint Peter's. Before I finished I said to myself "The fellow's a bankrupt orange-monger, but a treasure."

When Mrs. Monarch withdrew he passed across the room like a flash to open the door for her, standing there with the rapt pure gaze of the young Dante spellbound by the young Beatrice. As I never insisted, in such situations, on the blankness of the British domestic, I reflected that he had the making of a servant--and I needed one, but couldn't pay him to be only that--as well as of a model; in short I resolved to adopt my bright adventurer if he would agree to officiate in the double capacity. He jumped at my offer, and in the event my rashness--for I had really known nothing about him--wasn't brought home to me. He proved a sympathetic though a desultory ministrant, and had in a wonderful degree the sentiment de la pose. It was uncultivated, instinctive, a part of the happy instinct that had guided him to my door and helped him to spell out my name on the card nailed to it. He had had no other introduction to me than a guess, from the shape of my high north window, seen outside, that my place was a studio and that as a studio it would contain an artist. He had wandered to England in search of fortune, like other itinerants, and had embarked, with a partner and a small green hand-cart, on the sale of penny ices. The ices had melted away and the partner had dissolved in their train. My young man wore tight yellow trousers with reddish stripes and his name was Oronte. He was sallow but fair, and when I put him into some old clothes of my own he looked like an Englishman. He was as good as Miss Churm, who could look, when requested, like an Italian.

CHAPTER IV

I thought Mrs. Monarch's face slightly convulsed when, on her coming back with her husband, she found Oronte installed. It was strange to have to recognise in a scrap of a lazzarone a competitor to her magnificent Major. It was she who scented danger first, for the Major was anecdotically unconscious. But Oronte gave us tea, with a hundred eager confusions--he had never been concerned in so queer a process--and I think she thought better of me for having at last an "establishment." They saw a couple of drawings that I had made of the establishment, and Mrs. Monarch hinted that it never would have struck her he had sat for them. "Now the drawings you make from US, they look exactly like us," she reminded me, smiling in triumph; and I recognised that this was indeed just their defect. When I drew the Monarchs I couldn't anyhow get away from them--get into the character I wanted to represent; and I hadn't the least desire my model should be discoverable in my picture. Miss Churm never was, and Mrs. Monarch thought I hid her, very properly, because she was vulgar; whereas if she was lost it was only as the dead who go to heaven are lost--in the gain of an angel the more.

By this time I had got a certain start with "Rutland Ramsay," the first novel in the great projected series; that is I had produced a dozen drawings, several with the help of the Major and his wife, and I had sent them in for approval. My understanding with the publishers as I have already hinted, had been that I was to be left to do my work, in this particular case, as I liked, with the whole book committed to me; but my connexion with the rest of the series was only contingent. There were moments when, frankly, it WAS a comfort to have the real thing under one's hand for there were characters in "Rutland Ramsay" that were very much like it. There were people presumably as erect as the Major and women of as good a fashion as Mrs. Monarch. There was a great deal of country-house life-treated, it is true, in a fine fanciful ironical generalised way--and there was a considerable implication of knickerbockers and kilts. There were certain things I had to settle at the outset; such things for instance as the exact appearance of the hero and the particular bloom and figure of the heroine. The author of course gave me a lead, but there was a margin for interpretation. I took the Monarchs into my confidence, I told them frankly what I was about, I mentioned my embarrassments and alternatives. "Oh take HIM!" Mrs. Monarch murmured sweetly, looking at her husband; and "What could you want better than my wife?" the Major inquired with the comfortable candour that now prevailed between us.

I wasn't obliged to answer these remarks--I was only obliged to place my sitters. I wasn't easy in mind, and I postponed a little timidly perhaps the solving of my question. The book was a large canvas, the other figures were numerous, and I worked off at first some of the episodes in which the hero and the heroine were not concerned. When once I had set THEM up I should have to stick to them--I couldn't make my young man seven feet high in one place and five feet nine in another. I inclined on the whole to the latter measurement, though the Major more than once reminded me that he looked about as young as any one. It was indeed quite possible to arrange him, for the figure, so that it would have been difficult to detect his age. After the spontaneous Oronte had been with me a month, and after I had given him to understand several times over that his native exuberance would presently constitute an insurmountable barrier to our further intercourse, I waked to a sense of his heroic capacity. He was only five feet seven, but the remaining inches were latent. I tried him almost secretly at first, for I was really rather afraid of the judgement my other models would pass on such a choice. If they regarded Miss Churm as little better than a snare what would they think of the representation by a person so little the real thing as an Italian street-vendor of a protagonist formed by a public school?

If I went a little in fear of them it wasn't because they bullied me, because they had got an oppressive foothold, but because in their really pathetic decorum and mysteriously permanent newness they counted on me so intensely. I was therefore very glad when Jack Hawley came home: he was always of such good counsel. He painted badly himself, but there was no one like him for putting his finger on the place. He had been absent from England for a year; he had been somewhere--I don't remember where--to get a fresh eye. I was in a good deal of dread of any such organ, but we were old friends; he had been away for months and a sense of emptiness was creeping into my life. I hadn't dodged a missile for a year.

He came back with a fresh eye, but with the same old black velvet blouse, and the first evening he spent in my studio we smoked cigarettes till the small hours. He had done no work himself, he had only got the eye; so the field was clear for the production of my little things. He wanted to see what I had produced for the Cheapside, but he was disappointed in the exhibition. That at least seemed the meaning of two or three comprehensive groans which, as he lounged on my big divan, his leg folded under him, looking at my latest drawings, issued from his lips with the smoke of the cigarette.

"What's the matter with you?" I asked.

"What's the matter with you?"

"Nothing save that I'm mystified."

"You are indeed. You're quite off the hinge. What's the meaning of this new fad?" And he tossed me, with visible irreverence, a drawing in which I happened to have depicted both my elegant models. I asked if he didn't think it good, and he replied that it struck him as execrable, given the sort of thing I had always represented myself to him as wishing to arrive at; but I let that pass--I was so anxious to see exactly what he meant. The two figures in the picture looked colossal, but I supposed this was not what he meant, inasmuch as, for aught he knew to the contrary, I might have been trying for some such effect. I maintained that I was working exactly in the same way as when he last had done me the honour to tell me I might do something some day. "Well, there's a screw loose somewhere," he answered; "wait a bit and I'll discover it." I depended upon him to do so: where else was the fresh eye? But he produced at last nothing more luminous than "I don't know--I don't like your types." This was lame for a critic who had never consented to discuss with me anything but the question of execution, the direction of strokes and the mystery of values.

"In the drawings you've been looking at I think my types are very handsome."

"Oh they won't do!"

"I've been working with new models."

"I see you have. THEY won't do."

"Are you very sure of that?"

"Absolutely--they're stupid."

"You mean I am--for I ought to get round that."

"You can't--with such people. Who are they?"

I told him, so far as was necessary, and he concluded heartlessly: "Ce sont des gens qu'il faut mettre a la porte."

"You've never seen them; they're awfully good"--I flew to their defence.

"Not seen them? Why all this recent work of yours drops to pieces with them. It's all I want to see of them."

"No one else has said anything against it--the Cheapside people are pleased."

"Every one else is an ass, and the Cheapside people the biggest asses of all. Come, don't pretend at this time of day to have pretty illusions about the public, especially about publishers and editors. It's not for SUCH animals you work--it's for those who know, coloro che sanno; so keep straight for me if you can't keep straight for yourself. There was a certain sort of thing you used to try for--and a very good thing it was. But this twaddle isn't in it." When I talked with Hawley later about "Rutland Ramsay" and its possible successors he declared that I must get back into my boat again or I should go to the bottom. His voice in short was the voice of warning.

I noted the warning, but I didn't turn my friends out of doors. They bored me a good deal; but the very fact that they bored me admonished me not to sacrifice them--if there was anything to be done with them--simply to irritation. As I look back at this phase they seem to me to have pervaded my life not a little. I have a vision of them as most of the time in my studio, seated against the wall on an old velvet bench to be out of the way, and resembling the while a pair of patient courtiers in a royal antechamber. I'm convinced that during the coldest weeks of the winter they held their ground because it saved them fire. Their newness was losing its gloss, and it was impossible not to feel them objects of charity. Whenever Miss Churm arrived they went away, and after I was fairly launched in "Rutland Ramsay" Miss Churm arrived pretty often. They managed to express to me tacitly that they supposed I wanted her for the low life of the book, and I let them suppose it, since they had attempted to study the work--it was lying about the studio--without discovering that it dealt only with the highest circles. They had dipped into the most brilliant of our novelists without deciphering many passages. I still took an hour from them, now and again, in spite of Jack Hawley's warning: it would be time enough to dismiss them, if dismissal should be necessary, when the rigour of the season was over. Hawley had made their acquaintance- -he had met them at my fireside--and thought them a ridiculous pair. Learning that he was a painter they tried to approach him, to show him too that they were the real thing; but he looked at them across the big room, as if they were miles away: they were a compendium of everything he most objected to in the social system of his country. Such people as that, all convention and patent- leather, with ejaculations that stopped conversation, had no business in a studio. A studio was a place to learn to see, and how could you see through a pair of feather-beds?

The main inconvenience I suffered at their hands was that at first I was shy of letting it break upon them that my artful little servant had begun to sit to me for "Rutland Ramsay." They knew I had been odd enough--they were prepared by this time to allow oddity to artists--to pick a foreign vagabond out of the streets when I might have had a person with whiskers and credentials; but it was some time before they learned how high I rated his accomplishments. They found him in an attitude more than once, but they never doubted I was doing him as an organ-grinder. There were several things they never guessed, and one of them was that for a striking scene in the novel, in which a footman briefly figured, it occurred to me to make use of Major Monarch as the menial.

I kept putting this off, I didn't like to ask him to don the livery-- besides the difficulty of finding a livery to fit him. At last, one day late in the winter, when I was at work on the despised Oronte, who caught one's idea on the wing, and was in the glow of feeling myself go very straight, they came in, the Major and his wife, with their society laugh about nothing (there was less and less to laugh at); came in like country-callers--they always reminded me of that--who have walked across the park after church and are presently persuaded to stay to luncheon. Luncheon was over, but they could stay to tea--I knew they wanted it. The fit was on me, however, and I couldn't let my ardour cool and my work wait, with the fading daylight, while my model prepared it. So I asked Mrs. Monarch if she would mind laying it out--a request which for an instant brought all the blood to her face. Her eyes were on her husband's for a second, and some mute telegraphy passed between them. Their folly was over the next instant; his cheerful shrewdness put an end to it. So far from pitying their wounded pride, I must add, I was moved to give it as complete a lesson as I could. They bustled about together and got out the cups and saucers and made the kettle boil. I know they felt as if they were waiting on my servant, and when the tea was prepared I said: "He'll have a cup, please--he's tired." Mrs. Monarch brought him one where he stood, and he took it from her as if he had been a gentleman at a party squeezing a crush-hat with an elbow.

Then it came over me that she had made a great effort for me--made it with a kind of nobleness--and that I owed her a compensation. Each time I saw her after this I wondered what the compensation could be. I couldn't go on doing the wrong thing to oblige them. Oh it WAS the wrong thing, the stamp of the work for which they sat--Hawley was not the only person to say it now. I sent in a large number of the drawings I had made for "Rutland Ramsay," and I received a warning that was more to the point than Hawley's. The artistic adviser of the house for which I was working was of opinion that many of my illustrations were not what had been looked for. Most of these illustrations were the subjects in which the Monarchs had figured. Without going into the question of what HAD been looked for, I had to face the fact that at this rate I shouldn't get the other books to do. I hurled myself in despair on Miss Churm--I put her through all her paces. I not only adopted Oronte publicly as my hero, but one morning when the Major looked in to see if I didn't require him to finish a Cheapside figure for which he had begun to sit the week before, I told him I had changed my mind--I'd do the drawing from my man. At this my visitor turned pale and stood looking at me. "Is HE your idea of an English gentleman?" he asked.

I was disappointed, I was nervous, I wanted to get on with my work; so. I replied with irritation: "Oh my dear Major--I can't be ruined for YOU!"

It was a horrid speech, but he stood another moment--after which, without a word, he quitted the studio. I drew a long breath, for I said to myself that I shouldn't see him again. I hadn't told--him definitely that I was in danger of having my work rejected, but I was vexed at his not having felt the catastrophe in the air, read with me the moral of our fruitless collaboration, the lesson that in the deceptive atmosphere of art even the highest respectability may fail of being plastic.

I didn't owe my friends money, but I did see them again. They reappeared together three days later, and, given all the other facts, there was something tragic in that one. It was a clear proof they could find nothing else in life to do. They had threshed the matter out in a dismal conference--they had digested the bad news that they were not in for the series. If they weren't useful to me even for the Cheapside their function seemed difficult to determine, and I could only judge at first that they had come, forgivingly, decorously, to take a last leave. This made me rejoice in secret that I had little leisure for a scene; for I had placed both my other models in position together and I was pegging away at a drawing from which I hoped to derive glory. It had been suggested by the passage in -which Rutland Ramsay, drawing up a chair to Artemisia's piano-stool, says extraordinary things to her while she ostensibly fingers out a difficult piece of music. I had done Miss Churm at the piano before--it was an attitude in which she knew how to take on an absolutely poetic grace. I wished the two figures to "compose" together with intensity, and my little Italian had entered perfectly into my conception. The pair were vividly before me, the piano had been pulled out; it was a charming show of blended youth and murmured love, which I had only to catch and keep. My visitors stood and looked at it, and I was friendly to them over my shoulder.

They made no response, but I was used to silent company and went on with my work, only a little disconcerted--even though exhilarated by the sense that this was at least the ideal thing--at not having got rid of them after all. Presently I heard Mrs. Monarch's sweet voice beside or rather above me: "I wish her hair were a little better done." I looked up and she was staring with a strange fixedness at Miss Churm, whose back was turned to her. "Do you mind my just touching it?" she went on--a question which made me spring up for an instant as with the instinctive fear that she might do the young lady a harm. But she quieted me with a glance I shall never forget--I confess I should like to have been able to paint that--and went for a moment to my model. She spoke to her softly, laying a hand on her shoulder and bending over her; and as the girl, understanding, gratefully assented, she disposed her rough curls, with a few quick passes, in such a way as to make Miss Churm's head twice as charming. It was one of the most heroic personal services I've ever seen rendered. Then Mrs. Monarch turned away with a low sigh and, looking about her as if for something to do, stooped to the floor with a noble humility and picked up a dirty rag that had dropped out of my paint-box.

The Major meanwhile had also been looking for something to do, and, wandering to the other end of the studio, saw before him my breakfast-things neglected, unremoved. "I say, can't I be useful HERE?" he called out to me with an irrepressible quaver. I assented with a laugh that I fear was awkward, and for the next ten minutes, while I worked, I heard the light clatter of china and the tinkle of spoons and glass. Mrs. Monarch assisted her husband-- they washed up my crockery, they put it away. They wandered off into my little scullery, and I afterwards found that they had cleaned my knives and that my slender stock of plate had an unprecedented surface. When it came over me, the latent eloquence of what they were doing, I confess that my drawing was blurred for a moment--the picture swam. They had accepted their failure, but they couldn't accept their fate. They had bowed their heads in bewilderment to the perverse and cruel law in virtue of which the real thing could be so much less precious than the unreal; but they didn't want to starve. If my servants were my models, then my models might be my servants. They would reverse the parts--the others would sit for the ladies and gentlemen and THEY would do the work. They would still be in the studio--it was an intense dumb appeal to me not to turn them out. "Take us on," they wanted to say--"we'll do ANYTHING."

My pencil dropped from my hand; my sitting was spoiled and I got rid of my sitters, who were also evidently rather mystified and awestruck. Then, alone with the Major and his wife I had a most uncomfortable moment. He put their prayer into a single sentence: "I say, you know--just let US do for you, can't you?" I couldn't-- it was dreadful to see them emptying my slops; but I pretended I could, to oblige them, for about a week. Then I gave them a sum of money to go away, and I never saw them again. I obtained the remaining books, but my friend Hawley repeats that Major and Mrs. Monarch did me a permanent harm, got me into false ways. If it be true I'm content to have paid the price--for the memory.

THEFT - A SHORT STORY BY KATHERINE ANNE PORTER

can be read online at: http://www.questia.com/read/78267055?title=Flowering%20Judas%3a%20And%20Other%20Stories

YOUNG GOODMAN BROWN - A SHORT STORY BY NATHANIEL HAWTHORNE

Young Goodman Brown came forth at sunset into the street at Salem village; but put his head back, after crossing the threshold, to exchange a parting kiss with his young wife. And Faith, as the wife was aptly named, thrust her own pretty head into the street, letting the wind play with the pink ribbons of her cap while she called to Goodman Brown.

"Dearest heart," whispered she, softly and rather sadly, when her lips were close to his ear, "prithee put off your journey until sunrise and sleep in your own bed to-night. A lone woman is troubled with such dreams and such thoughts that she's afeard of herself sometimes. Pray tarry with me this night, dear husband, of all nights in the year."

"My love and my Faith," replied young Goodman Brown, "of all nights in the year, this one night must I tarry away from thee. My journey, as thou callest it, forth and back again, must needs be done 'twixt now and sunrise. What, my sweet, pretty wife, dost thou doubt me already, and we but three months married?"

"Then God bless youe!" said Faith, with the pink ribbons; "and may you find all well whn you come back."

"Amen!" cried Goodman Brown. "Say thy prayers, dear Faith, and go to bed at dusk, and no harm will come to thee."

So they parted; and the young man pursued his way until, being about to turn the corner by the meeting-house, he looked back and saw the head of Faith still peeping after him with a melancholy air, in spite of her pink ribbons.

"Poor little Faith!" thought he, for his heart smote him. "What a wretch am I to leave her on such an errand! She talks of dreams, too. Methought as she spoke there was trouble in her face, as if a dream had warned her what work is to be done tonight. But no, no; 't would kill her to think it. Well, she's a blessed angel on earth; and after this one night I'll cling to her skirts and follow her to heaven."

With this excellent resolve for the future, Goodman Brown felt himself justified in making more haste on his present evil purpose. He had taken a dreary road, darkened by all the gloomiest trees of the forest, which barely stood aside to let the narrow path creep through, and closed immediately behind. It was all as lonely as could be; and there is this peculiarity in such a solitude, that the traveller knows not who may be concealed by the innumerable trunks and the thick boughs overhead; so that with lonely footsteps he may yet be passing through an unseen multitude.

"There may be a devilish Indian behind every tree," said Goodman Brown to himself; and he glanced fearfully behind him as he added, "What if the devil himself should be at my very elbow!"

His head being turned back, he passed a crook of the road, and, looking forward again, beheld the figure of a man, in grave and decent attire, seated at the foot of an old tree. He arose at Goodman Brown's approach and walked onward side by side with him.

"You are late, Goodman Brown," said he. "The clock of the Old South was striking as I came through Boston, and that is full fifteen minutes agone."

"Faith kept me back a while," replied the young man, with a tremor in his voice, caused by the sudden appearance of his companion, though not wholly unexpected.

It was now deep dusk in the forest, and deepest in that part of it where these two were journeying. As nearly as could be discerned, the second traveller was about fifty years old, apparently in the same rank of life as Goodman Brown, and bearing a considerable resemblance to him, though perhaps more in expression than features. Still they might have been taken for father and son. And yet, though the elder person was as simply clad as the younger, and as simple in manner too, he had an indescribable air of one who knew the world, and who would not have felt abashed at the governor's dinner table or in King William's court, were it possible that his affairs should call him thither. But the only thing about him that could be fixed upon as remarkable was his staff, which bore the likeness of a great black snake, so curiously wrought that it might almost be seen to twist and wriggle itself like a living serpent. This, of course, must have been an ocular deception, assisted by the uncertain light.

"Come, Goodman Brown," cried his fellow-traveller, "this is a dull pace for the beginning of a journey. Take my staff, if you are so soon weary."

"Friend," said the other, exchanging his slow pace for a full stop, "having kept covenant by meeting thee here, it is my purpose now to return whence I came. I have scruples touching the matter thou wot'st of."

"Sayest thou so?" replied he of the serpent, smiling apart. "Let us walk on, nevertheless, reasoning as we go; and if I convince thee not thou shalt turn back. We are but a little way in the forest yet."

"Too far! too far!" exclaimed the goodman, unconsciously resuming his walk. "My father never went into the woods on such an errand, nor his father before him. We have been a race of honest men and good Christians since the days of the martyrs; and shall I be the first of the name of Brown that ever took this path and kept"

"Such company, thou wouldst say," observed the elder person, interpreting his pause. "Well said, Goodman Brown! I have been as well acquainted with your family as with ever a one among the Puritans; and that's no trifle to say. I helped your grandfather, the constable, when he lashed the Quaker woman so smartly through the streets of Salem; and it was I that brought your father a pitch-pine knot, kindled at my own hearth, to set fire to an Indian village, in King Philip's war. They were my good friends, both; and many a pleasant walk have we had along this path, and returned merrily after midnight. I would fain be friends with you for their sake."

"If it be as thou sayest," replied Goodman Brown, "I marvel they never spoke of these matters; or, verily, I marvel not, seeing that the least rumor of the sort would have driven them from New England. We are a people of prayer, and good works to boot, and abide no such wickedness."

"Wickedness or not," said the traveller with the twisted staff, "I have a very general acquaintance here in New England. The deacons of many a church have drunk the communion wine with me; the selectmen of divers towns make me their chairman; and a majority of the Great and General Court are firm supporters of my interest. The governor and I, too--But these are state secrets."

"Can this be so?" cried Goodman Brown, with a stare of amazement at his undisturbed companion. "Howbeit, I have nothing to do with the governor and council; they have their own ways, and are no rule for a simple husbandman like me. But, were I to go on with thee, how should I meet the eye of that good old man, our minister, at Salem village? Oh, his voice would make me tremble both Sabbath day and lecture day."

Thus far the elder traveller had listened with due gravity; but now burst into a fit of irrepressible mirth, shaking himself so violently that his snake-like staff actually seemed to wriggle in sympathy.

"Ha! ha! ha!" shouted he again and again; then composing himself, "Well, go on, Goodman Brown, go on; but, prithee, don't kill me with laughing."

"Well, then, to end the matter at once," said Goodman Brown, considerably nettled, "there is my wife, Faith. It would break her dear little heart; and I'd rather break my own."

"Nay, if that be the case," answered the other, "e'en go thy ways, Goodman Brown. I would not for twenty old women like the one hobbling before us that Faith should come to any harm."

As he spoke he pointed his staff at a female figure on the path, in whom Goodman Brown recognized a very pious and exemplary dame, who had taught him his catechism in youth, and was still his moral and spiritual adviser, jointly with the minister and Deacon Gookin.

"A marvel, truly, that Goody Cloyse should be so far in the wilderness at nightfall," said he. "But with your leave, friend, I shall take a cut through the woods until we have left this Christian woman behind. Being a stranger to you, she might ask whom I was consorting with and whither I was going."

"Be it so," said his fellow-traveller. "Betake you to the woods, and let me keep the path."

Accordingly the young man turned aside, but took care to watch his companion, who advanced softly along the road until he had come within a staff's length of the old dame. She, meanwhile, was making the best of her way, with singular speed for so aged a woman, and mumbling some indistinct words--a prayer, doubtless--as she went. The traveller put forth his staff and touched her withered neck with what seemed the serpent's tail.

"The devil!" screamed the pious old lady.

"Then Goody Cloyse knows her old friend?" observed the traveller, confronting her and leaning on his writhing stick.

"Ah, forsooth, and is it your worship indeed?" cried the good dame. "Yea, truly is it, and in the very image of my old gossip, Goodman Brown, the grandfather of the silly fellow that now is. But--would your worship believe it?--my broomstick hath strangely disappeared, stolen, as I suspect, by that unhanged witch, Goody Cory, and that, too, when I was all anointed with the juice of smallage, and cinquefoil, and wolf's bane"

"Mingled with fine wheat and the fat of a new-born babe," said the shape of old Goodman Brown.

"Ah, your worship knows the recipe," cried the old lady, cackling aloud. "So, as I was saying, being all ready for the meeting, and no horse to ride on, I made up my mind to foot it; for they tell me there is a nice young man to be taken into communion to-night. But now your good worship will lend me your arm, and we shall be there in a twinkling."

"That can hardly be," answered her friend. "I may not spare you my arm, Goody Cloyse; but here is my staff, if you will."

So saying, he threw it down at her feet, where, perhaps, it assumed life, being one of the rods which its owner had formerly lent to the Egyptian magi. Of this fact, however, Goodman Brown could not take cognizance. He had cast up his eyes in astonishment, and, looking down again, beheld neither Goody Cloyse nor the serpentine staff, but his fellow-traveller alone, who waited for him as calmly as if nothing had happened.

"That old woman taught me my catechism," said the young man; and there was a world of meaning in this simple comment.

They continued to walk onward, while the elder traveller exhorted his companion to make good speed and persevere in the path, discoursing so aptly that his arguments seemed rather to spring up in the bosom of his auditor than to be suggested by himself. As they went, he plucked a branch of maple to serve for a walking stick, and began to strip it of the twigs and little boughs, which were wet with evening dew. The moment his fingers touched them they became strangely withered and dried up as with a week's sunshine. Thus the pair proceeded, at a good free pace, until suddenly, in a gloomy hollow of the road, Goodman Brown sat himself down on the stump of a tree and refused to go any farther.

"Friend," said he, stubbornly, "my mind is made up. Not another step will I budge on this errand. What if a wretched old woman do choose to go to the devil when I thought she was going to heaven: is that any reason why I should quit my dear Faith and go after her?"

"You will think better of this by and by," said his acquaintance, composedly. "Sit here and rest yourself a while; and when you feel like moving again, there is my staff to help you along."

Without more words, he threw his companion the maple stick, and was as speedily out of sight as if he had vanished into the deepening gloom. The young man sat a few moments by the roadside, applauding himself greatly, and thinking with how clear a conscience he should meet the minister in his morning walk, nor shrink from the eye of good old Deacon Gookin. And what calm sleep would be his that very night, which was to have been spent so wickedly, but so purely and sweetly now, in the arms of Faith! Amidst these pleasant and praiseworthy meditations, Goodman Brown heard the tramp of horses along the road, and deemed it advisable to conceal himself within the verge of the forest, conscious of the guilty purpose that had brought him thither, though now so happily turned from it.

On came the hoof tramps and the voices of the riders, two grave old voices, conversing soberly as they drew near. These mingled sounds appeared to pass along the road, within a few yards of the young man's hiding-place; but, owing doubtless to the depth of the gloom at that particular spot, neither the travellers nor their steeds were visible. Though their figures brushed the small boughs by the wayside, it could not be seen that they intercepted, even for a moment, the faint gleam from the strip of bright sky athwart which they must have passed. Goodman Brown alternately crouched and stood on tiptoe, pulling aside the branches and thrusting forth his head as far as he durst without discerning so much as a shadow. It vexed him the more, because he could have sworn, were such a thing possible, that he recognized the voices of the minister and Deacon Gookin, jogging along quietly, as they were wont to do, when bound to some ordination or ecclesiastical council. While yet within hearing, one of the riders stopped to pluck a switch.

"Of the two, reverend sir," said the voice like the deacon's, "I had rather miss an ordination dinner than to-night's meeting. They tell me that some of our community are to be here from Falmouth and beyond, and others from Connecticut and Rhode Island, besides several of the Indian powwows, who, after their fashion, know almost as much deviltry as the best of us. Moreover, there is a goodly young woman to be taken into communion."

"Mighty well, Deacon Gookin!" replied the solemn old tones of the minister. "Spur up, or we shall be late. Nothing can be done, you know, until I get on the ground."

The hoofs clattered again; and the voices, talking so strangely in the empty air, passed on through the forest, where no church had ever been gathered or solitary Christian prayed. Whither, then, could these holy men be journeying so deep into the heathen wilderness? Young Goodman Brown caught hold of a tree for support, being ready to sink down on the ground, faint and overburdened with the heavy sickness of his heart. He looked up to the sky, doubting whether there really was a heaven above him. Yet there was the blue arch, and the stars brightening in it.

"With heaven above and Faith below, I will yet stand firm against the devil!" cried Goodman Brown.

While he still gazed upward into the deep arch of the firmament and had lifted his hands to pray, a cloud, though no wind was stirring, hurried across the zenith and hid the brightening stars. The blue sky was still visible, except directly overhead, where this black mass of cloud was sweeping swiftly northward. Aloft in the air, as if from the depths of the cloud, came a confused and doubtful sound of voices. Once the listener fancied that he could distinguish the accents of towns-people of his own, men and women, both pious and ungodly, many of whom he had met at the communion table, and had seen others rioting at the tavern. The next moment, so indistinct were the sounds, he doubted whether he had heard aught but the murmur of the old forest, whispering without a wind. Then came a stronger swell of those familiar tones, heard daily in the sunshine at Salem village, but never until now from a cloud of night There was one voice of a young woman, uttering lamentations, yet with an uncertain sorrow, and entreating for some favor, which, perhaps, it would grieve her to obtain; and all the unseen multitude, both saints and sinners, seemed to encourage her onward.

"Faith!" shouted Goodman Brown, in a voice of agony and desperation; and the echoes of the forest mocked him, crying, "Faith! Faith!" as if bewildered wretches were seeking her all through the wilderness.

The cry of grief, rage, and terror was yet piercing the night, when the unhappy husband held his breath for a response. There was a scream, drowned immediately in a louder murmur of voices, fading into far-off laughter, as the dark cloud swept away, leaving the clear and silent sky above Goodman Brown. But something fluttered lightly down through the air and caught on the branch of a tree. The young man seized it, and beheld a pink ribbon.

"My Faith is gone!" cried he, after one stupefied moment. "There is no good on earth; and sin is but a name. Come, devil; for to thee is this world given."

And, maddened with despair, so that he laughed loud and long, did Goodman Brown grasp his staff and set forth again, at such a rate that he seemed to fly along the forest path rather than to walk or run. The road grew wilder and drearier and more faintly traced, and vanished at length, leaving him in the heart of the dark wilderness, still rushing onward with the instinct that guides mortal man to evil. The whole forest was peopled with frightful sounds--the creaking of the trees, the howling of wild beasts, and the yell of Indians; while sometimes the wind tolled like a distant church bell, and sometimes gave a broad roar around the traveller, as if all Nature were laughing him to scorn. But he was himself the chief horror of the scene, and shrank not from its other horrors.

"Ha! ha! ha!" roared Goodman Brown when the wind laughed at him.

"Let us hear which will laugh loudest. Think not to frighten me with your deviltry. Come witch, come wizard, come Indian powwow, come devil himself, and here comes Goodman Brown. You may as well fear him as he fear you."

In truth, all through the haunted forest there could be nothing more frightful than the figure of Goodman Brown. On he flew among the black pines, brandishing his staff with frenzied gestures, now giving vent to an inspiration of horrid blasphemy, and now shouting forth such laughter as set all the echoes of the forest laughing like demons around him. The fiend in his own shape is less hideous than when he rages in the breast of man. Thus sped the demoniac on his course, until, quivering among the trees, he saw a red light before him, as when the felled trunks and branches of a clearing have been set on fire, and throw up their lurid blaze against the sky, at the hour of midnight. He paused, in a lull of the tempest that had driven him onward, and heard the swell of what seemed a hymn, rolling solemnly from a distance with the weight of many voices. He knew the tune; it was a familiar one in the choir of the village meeting-house. The verse died heavily away, and was lengthened by a chorus, not of human voices, but of all the sounds of the benighted wilderness pealing in awful harmony together. Goodman Brown cried out, and his cry was lost to his own ear by its unison with the cry of the desert.

In the interval of silence he stole forward until the light glared full upon his eyes. At one extremity of an open space, hemmed in by the dark wall of the forest, arose a rock, bearing some rude, natural resemblance either to an alter or a pulpit, and surrounded by four blazing pines, their tops aflame, their stems untouched, like candles at an evening meeting. The mass of foliage that had overgrown the summit of the rock was all on fire, blazing high into the night and fitfully illuminating the whole field. Each pendent twig and leafy festoon was in a blaze. As the red light arose and fell, a numerous congregation alternately shone forth, then disappeared in shadow, and again grew, as it were, out of the darkness, peopling the heart of the solitary woods at once.

"A grave and dark-clad company," quoth Goodman Brown.

In truth they were such. Among them, quivering to and fro between gloom and splendor, appeared faces that would be seen next day at the council board of the province, and others which, Sabbath after Sabbath, looked devoutly heavenward, and benignantly over the crowded pews, from the holiest pulpits in the land. Some affirm that the lady of the governor was there. At least there were high dames well known to her, and wives of honored husbands, and widows, a great multitude, and ancient maidens, all of excellent repute, and fair young girls, who trembled lest their mothers should espy them. Either the sudden gleams of light flashing over the obscure field bedazzled Goodman Brown, or he recognized a score of the church members of Salem village famous for their especial sanctity. Good old Deacon Gookin had arrived, and waited at the skirts of that venerable saint, his revered pastor. But, irreverently consorting with these grave, reputable, and pious people, these elders of the church, these chaste dames and dewy virgins, there were men of dissolute lives and women of spotted fame, wretches given over to all mean and filthy vice, and suspected even of horrid crimes. It was strange to see that the good shrank not from the wicked, nor were the sinners abashed by the saints. Scattered also among their pale-faced enemies were the Indian priests, or pow-wows, who had often scared their native forest with more hideous incantations than any known to English witchcraft.

"But where is Faith?" thought Goodman Brown; and, as hope came into his heart, he trembled.

Another verse of the hymn arose, a slow and mournful strain, such as the pious love, but joined to words which expressed all that our nature can conceive of sin, and darkly hinted at far more. Unfathomable to mere mortals is the lore of fiends. Verse after verse was sung; and still the chorus of the desert swelled between like the deepest tone of a mighty organ; and with the final peal of that dreadful anthem there came a sound, as if the roaring wind, the rushing streams, the howling beasts, and every other voice of the unconcerted wilderness were mingling and according with the voice of guilty man in homage to the prince of all. The four blazing pines threw up a loftier flame, and obscurely discovered shapes and visages of horror on the smoke wreaths above the impious assembly. At the same moment the fire on the rock shot redly forth and formed a glowing arch above its base, where now appeared a figure. With reverence be it spoken, the figure bore no slight similitude, both in garb and manner, to some grave divine of the New England churches.

"Bring forth the converts!" cried a voice that echoed through the field and rolled into the forest.

At the word, Goodman Brown stepped forth from the shadow of the trees and approached the congregation, with whom he felt a loathful brotherhood by the sympathy of all that was wicked in his heart. He could have well-nigh sworn that the shape of his own dead father beckoned him to advance, looking downward from a smoke wreath, while a woman, with dim features of despair, threw out her hand to warn him back. Was it his mother? But he had no power to retreat one step, nor to resist, even in thought, when the minister and good old Deacon Gookin seized his arms and led him to the blazing rock. Thither came also the slender form of a veiled female, led between Goody Cloyse, that pious teacher of the catechism, and Martha Carrier, who had received the devil's promise to be queen of hell. A rampant hag was she. And there stood the proselytes beneath the canopy of fire.

"Welcome, my children," said the dark figure, "to the communion of your race. Ye have found thus young your nature and your destiny. My children, look behind you!"

They turned; and flashing forth, as it were, in a sheet of flame, the fiend worshippers were seen; the smile of welcome gleamed darkly on every visage.

"There," resumed the sable form, "are all whom ye have reverenced from youth. Ye deemed them holier than yourselves, and shrank from your own sin, contrasting it with their lives of righteousness and prayerful aspirations heavenward. Yet here are they all in my worshipping assembly. This night it shall be granted you to know their secret deeds: how hoary-bearded elders of the church have whispered wanton words to the young maids of their households; how many a woman, eager for widows' weeds, has given her husband a drink at bedtime and let him sleep his last sleep in her bosom; how beardless youths have made haste to inherit their fathers' wealth; and how fair damsels--blush not, sweet ones--have dug little graves in the garden, and bidden me, the sole guest to an infant's funeral. By the sympathy of your human hearts for sin ye shall scent out all the places--whether in church, bedchamber, street, field, or forest--where crime has been committed, and shall exult to behold the whole earth one stain of guilt, one mighty blood spot. Far more than this. It shall be yours to penetrate, in every bosom, the deep mystery of sin, the fountain of all wicked arts, and which inexhaustibly supplies more evil impulses than human power--than my power at its utmost--can make manifest in deeds. And now, my children, look upon each other."

They did so; and, by the blaze of the hell-kindled torches, the wretched man beheld his Faith, and the wife her husband, trembling before that unhallowed altar.

"Lo, there ye stand, my children," said the figure, in a deep and solemn tone, almost sad with its despairing awfulness, as if his once angelic nature could yet mourn for our miserable race. "Depending upon one another's hearts, ye had still hoped that virtue were not all a dream. Now are ye undeceived. Evil is the nature of mankind. Evil must be your only happiness. Welcome again, my children, to the communion of your race."

"Welcome," repeated the fiend worshippers, in one cry of despair and triumph.

And there they stood, the only pair, as it seemed, who were yet hesitating on the verge of wickedness in this dark world. A basin was hollowed, naturally, in the rock. Did it contain water, reddened by the lurid light? or was it blood? or, perchance, a liquid flame? Herein did the shape of evil dip his hand and prepare to lay the mark of baptism upon their foreheads, that they might be partakers of the mystery of sin, more conscious of the secret guilt of others, both in deed and thought, than they could now be of their own. The husband cast one look at his pale wife, and Faith at him. What polluted wretches would the next glance show them to each other, shuddering alike at what they disclosed and what they saw!

"Faith! Faith!" cried the husband, "look up to heaven, and resist the wicked one."

Whether Faith obeyed he knew not. Hardly had he spoken when he found himself amid calm night and solitude, listening to a roar of the wind which died heavily away through the forest. He staggered against the rock, and felt it chill and damp; while a hanging twig, that had been all on fire, besprinkled his cheek with the coldest dew.

The next morning young Goodman Brown came slowly into the street of Salem village, staring around him like a bewildered man. The good old minister was taking a walk along the graveyard to get an appetite for breakfast and meditate his sermon, and bestowed a blessing, as he passed, on Goodman Brown. He shrank from the venerable saint as if to avoid an anathema. Old Deacon Gookin was at domestic worship, and the holy words of his prayer were heard through the open window. "What God doth the wizard pray to?" quoth Goodman Brown. Goody Cloyse, that excellent old Christian, stood in the early sunshine at her own lattice, catechizing a little girl who had brought her a pint of morning's milk. Goodman Brown snatched away the child as from the grasp of the fiend himself. Turning the corner by the meeting-house, he spied the head of Faith, with the pink ribbons, gazing anxiously forth, and bursting into such joy at sight of him that she skipped along the street and almost kissed her husband before the whole village. But Goodman Brown looked sternly and sadly into her face, and passed on without a greeting.

Had Goodman Brown fallen asleep in the forest and only dreamed a wild dream of a witch-meeting?

Be it so if you will; but, alas! it was a dream of evil omen for young Goodman Brown. A stern, a sad, a darkly meditative, a distrustful, if not a desperate man did he become from the night of that fearful dream. On the Sabbath day, when the congregation were singing a holy psalm, he could not listen because an anthem of sin rushed loudly upon his ear and drowned all the blessed strain. When the minister spoke from the pulpit with power and fervid eloquence, and, with his hand on the open Bible, of the sacred truths of our religion, and of saint-like lives and triumphant deaths, and of future bliss or misery unutterable, then did Goodman Brown turn pale, dreading lest the roof should thunder down upon the gray blasphemer and his hearers. Often, waking suddenly at midnight, he shrank from the bosom of Faith; and at morning or eventide, when the family knelt down at prayer, he scowled and muttered to himself, and gazed sternly at his wife, and turned away. And when he had lived long, and was borne to his grave a hoary corpse, followed by Faith, an aged woman, and children and grandchildren, a goodly procession, besides neighbors not a few, they carved no hopeful verse upon his tombstone, for his dying hour was gloom.

FLASHCARDS

This section contains flashcards for you to use to further your understanding of the material and test yourself on important concepts, names or dates. Read the term or question then flip the page over to check the answer on the back. Keep in mind that this information may not be covered in the text of the study guide. Take your time to study the flashcards, you will need to know and understand these concepts to pass the test.

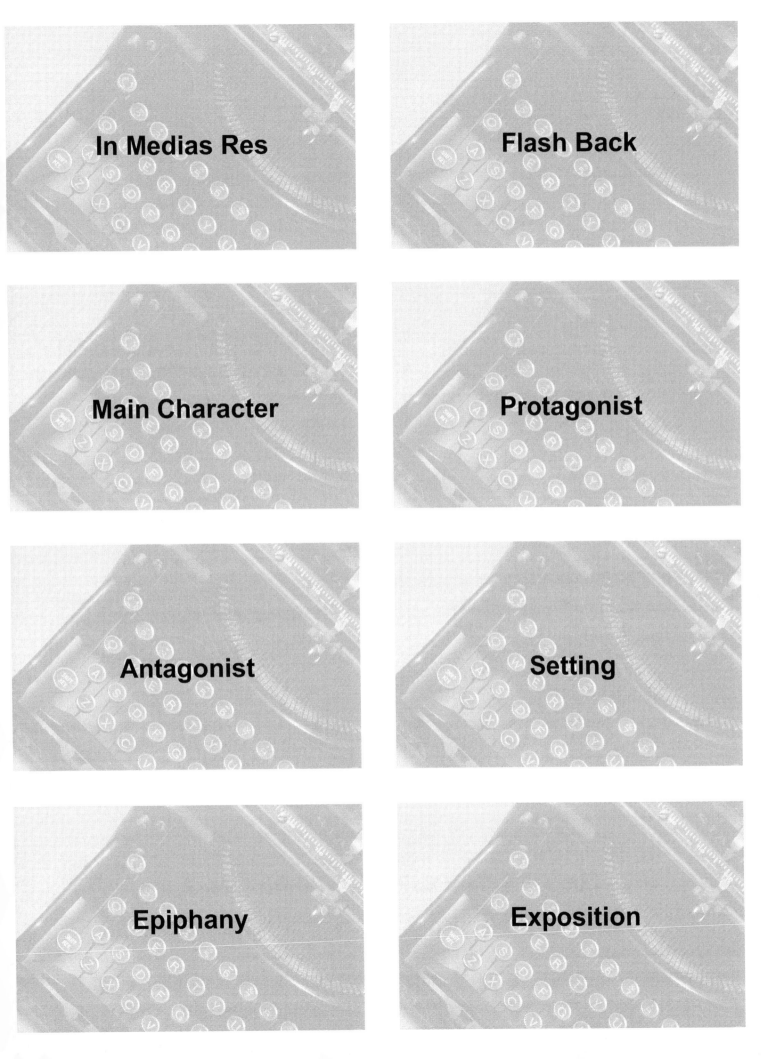

When the story goes back
in time

When a story starts in the
middle of an action

Another name for main
character

The primary character in a
story

Time, location or place
where a story takes place

The adversary or opponent

Where a reader meets the
characters and settings

When a character has a
sudden realization

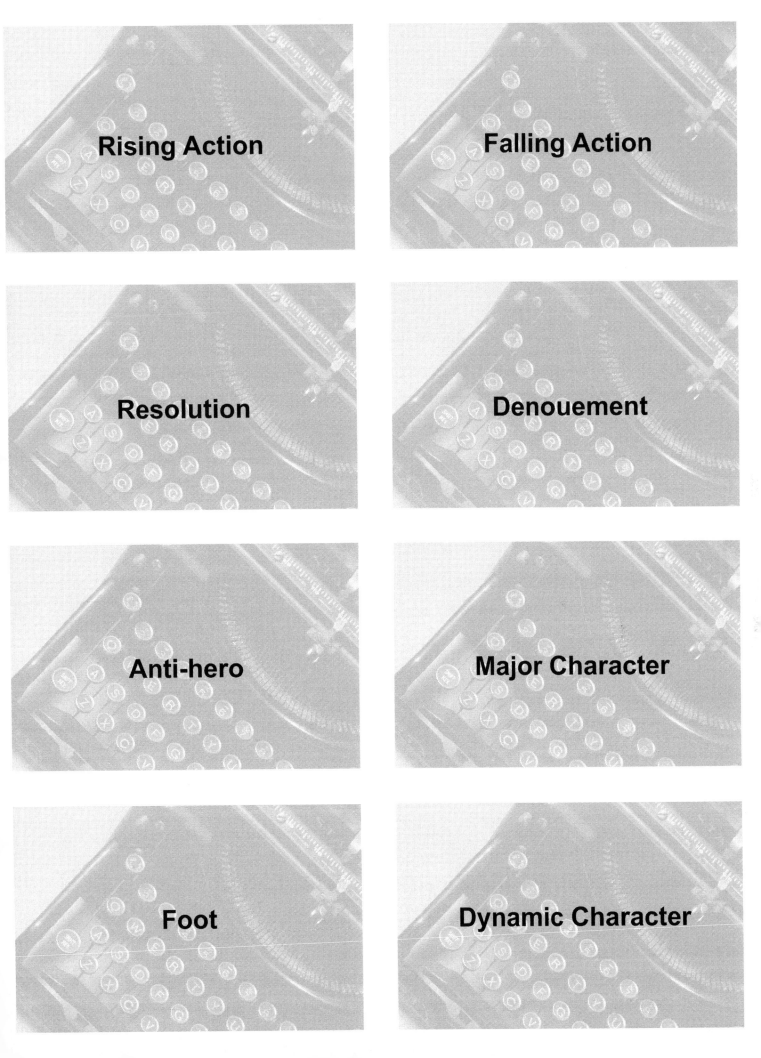

Rising Action

Falling Action

Resolution

Denouement

Anti-hero

Major Character

Foot

Dynamic Character

What happens after the climax

Where the reader finds out about the conflict and includes new problems

What happens after the climax

What happens after the climax

A character the story is focused on

A protagonist that doesn't have the noble characteristics that would make him a hero

A character that changes during the story

A combination of two or more syllables which form a unit of rhythm

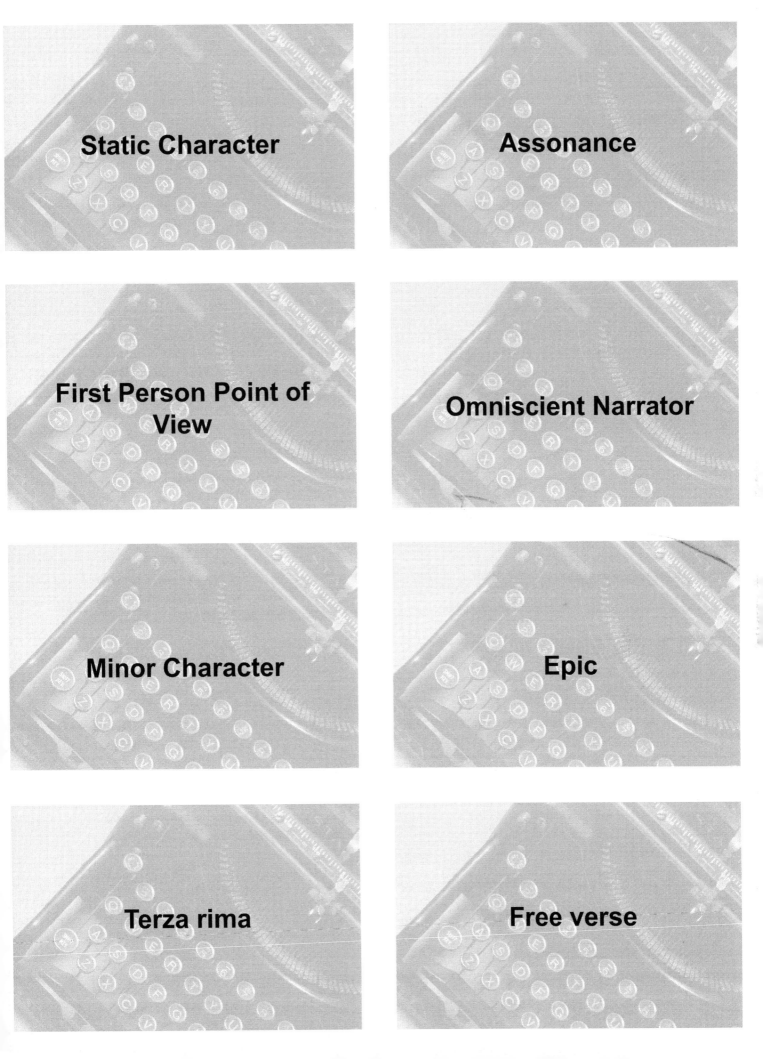

Static Character

Assonance

First Person Point of View

Omniscient Narrator

Minor Character

Epic

Terza rima

Free verse

Repetition of vowel sounds

A stable character that does not change during the story

This narrator can see inside the mind of all the characters of a story

A viewpoint from inside of a character

Long narrative poem

A supporting character

A style of poetry that has no set qualifications

A series of tercets which are linked together using chain rhyme

Made in the USA
Columbia, SC
08 April 2021